$1.95 EACH—WESTERN T

WARD RITCHIE PRESS

Trips for the Day, Week-end or Longer

ALL BOOKS COMPLETE WITH MANY PHOTOGRAPHS AND MAPS

QUANTITY		TOTAL
☐	A GUIDEBOOK TO THE SAN GABRIEL MOUNTAINS OF CALIFORNIA	$ _____
☐	A GUIDEBOOK TO THE SAN BERNARDINO MOUNTAINS OF CALIFORNIA, Including Lake Arrowhead and Big Bear	$ _____
☐	A GUIDEBOOK TO THE SAN JACINTO MOUNTAINS OF CALIFORNIA	$ _____
☐	A GUIDEBOOK TO THE MOUNTAINS OF SAN DIEGO AND RIVERSIDE COUNTIES	$ _____
☐	A GUIDEBOOK TO THE MOJAVE DESERT OF CALIFORNIA, Including Death Valley, Joshua Tree National Monument, and the Antelope Valley	$ _____
☐	A GUIDEBOOK TO THE SOUTHERN SIERRA NEVADA, Including Sequoia National Forest	$ _____
☐	A GUIDEBOOK TO RURAL CALIFORNIA	$ _____
☐	A GUIDEBOOK TO THE NORTHERN CALIFORNIA COAST, VOL. I. Highway 1	$ _____
☐	A GUIDEBOOK TO THE NORTHERN CALIFORNIA COAST, VOL. II. Humboldt and Del Norte Counties	$ _____
☐	A GUIDEBOOK TO THE LAKE TAHOE COUNTRY, VOL. 1. Echo Summit, Squaw Valley and the California Shore.	$ _____
☐	A GUIDEBOOK TO THE LAKE TAHOE COUNTRY, VOL. II. Alpine County, Donner-Truckee, and the Nevada Shore.	$ _____
☐	EXPLORING CALIFORNIA BYWAYS, #1 From Kings Canyon to the Mexican Border	$ _____
☐	EXPLORING CALIFORNIA BYWAYS, #2 In and Around Los Angeles	$ _____
☐	EXPLORING CALIFORNIA BYWAYS, #3 Desert Country	$ _____
☐	EXPLORING CALIFORNIA BYWAYS, #4 Mountain Country	$ _____

[SEE MORE BOOKS AND ORDER FORM ON OTHER SIDE]

☐	**EXPLORING CALIFORNIA BYWAYS, #5** Historic Sites of California	$ _____
☐	**EXPLORING CALIFORNIA BYWAYS, #6** Owens Valley	$ _____
☐	**WHERE TO TAKE YOUR CHILDREN IN SOUTHERN CALIFORNIA**	$ _____
☐	**WHERE TO TAKE YOUR CHILDREN IN NORTHERN CALIFORNIA**	$ _____
☐	**BICYCLE TOURING IN LOS ANGELES**	$ _____
☐	**YOUR LEISURE TIME . . . HOW TO ENJOY IT**	$ _____
☐	**NATURE AND THE CAMPER.** A Guide to Safety and Enjoyment for Campers and Hikers in the West.	$ _____
☐	**TREES OF THE WEST:** Identified at a Glance.	$ _____

WARD RITCHIE PRESS
3044 Riverside Drive, Los Angeles, Calif. 90039

Please send me the Western Travel Books I have checked. I am enclosing
$_____, (check or money order). Please include 25¢ per copy to cover
mailing costs. California residents add 5% sales tax.

Name _____

Address _____

City _____ State _____ Zip Code _____

RUSS LEADABRAND, veteran Southern California news-paperman and magazine writer, has been authoring guide-books and travel books for the Ward Ritchie Press since the early 1960s. He is also the travel editor of the Ward Ritchie travel and leisure paperbacks, busily at work on many new titles covering all sections of the West.

Leadabrand has driven and explored and researched all of the state of California and has described and photographed it for newspapers, magazines and his many travel books. He has traveled widely throughout the Pacific and South-west states as well as many other parts of the world.

*By winter snow is a frequent visitor to Rands-
burg. This picture was taken around 1900. Note
the many tent buildings.*

EXPLORING CALIFORNIA BYWAYS

III · *Desert Country*

Trips for a day or a weekend

BY RUSS LEADABRAND

THE WARD RITCHIE PRESS · LOS ANGELES

Based on a series of articles by *Russ Leadabrand*.
Originally published in *Westways*,
the official Publication of the
Automobile Club of Southern California.
Revised by Russ Leadabrand, 1969

Second Printing, March 1972

The material in this book is reviewed and updated
at each printing.

FOR LAURIE
*She hears a different drummer
but I have listened to him and
his beat is clear and reassuring.*

COVER PHOTO: *A sunset view of the Oasis of Mara at Twentynine Palms.
Color photo by Harold O. Weight.*

BACK COVER: *One of the little cliff-guarded canyons off the new
Truckhaven Trail in the Anza-Borrego Desert State Park.*

CONTENTS

PREFACE

Some people are city people—city people born or bred, or both. Take them away from concrete and steel and crowded thoroughfares and they are lost, unhappy.

Many more people are country lovers, and even though livelihood or other considerations may base them in the city, their hearts—occasionally, if not always—are away from it all.

Among the country people there are mountain people who worship thin air and the tang of pine needles; sea-coast adherents, uncomfortable when beyond the sight of combers and the scent of brine; and then there are champions of the desert, a strange breed that finds the desert's austerity, extremes and general stinginess with life a great attraction.

Country people usually favor one area to the neglect of the other two. Yet, Russ Leadabrand is an exception to this rule. For ten years I have known him as a man who is equally happy in all three settings. If I had to assign him a preference, however, it would be the desert.

Russ knows the desert. He knows the high and the low of it, its different diurnal and seasonal characters. He knows the slumbering ghost towns of the Mojave and the ancient Indian trails of the Colorado. He knows the mining lore of the painted Panamint Range, the wonder of a belly flower blooming in the Anza-Borrego by spring, and where Indian petroglyphs can be found.

Above all, Russ knows the byways that criss-cross southern California's vast arid interior.

This third volume of byway adventures will certainly please the confirmed desert lover. In it he will find much that is familiar and, no doubt, a good deal that is pleasingly new. For the reader indifferent to the desert—or perhaps even the inveterate desert-hater—there is a certain risk involved: he may very well find himself converted. Russ is a quiet though persuasive evangelist.

LARRY L. MEYER

INTRODUCTION

The California desert sings songs to me that no manner of ear-stoppering would ever prevent me from hearing. Or answering. When I suffer the wounds of city living, the small won't-heal cuts of too much pavement, too much ticky-tacky, too much iron and cement against the sky, I skitter away from it. I follow a wide road that becomes a narrow road that becomes a dirt road that becomes no road at all and then I keep driving until the desert wind tells me that at last I'm safe or the car just won't go any farther.

The desert is my security blanket. I seek it out in the winter, and I poke out into in the summer and fry and simmer and come home with the bad juices cooked out and only the burn on my nose and backs of hands to remind me that the medicine was strong.

The desert is too much sky and too much silence, it is too much horizon and too much nothing; it is reassuring in these excesses. I am one with the infinite when I can walk, head down, in a desert wind, and look for arrowheads on an ancient shoreline in the desert. I am whole when I am searching for bits of agate or fossils or bottles or railroad spikes or yesterday harness along a aqueduct camp route.

I invite the novices to the desert by wildflower time. The desert is bright then, it is reassuring. I hope that people who come when the desert is purple and gold and blue and white will come again when it is dun and sand and ochre and earth colors.

"Come to the desert when it is lonely, so lonely that you can feel it. It's like a poultice, it isn't doing you any good unless you can feel it," I tell them. Not everyone. Some are built of such a pattern that the tall sky and the horizon you cannot ever reach and the no marks of man stuff frightens them. They should steer clear of it. Enjoy the wildflowers and the old mine headframes and the ghosting towns and not venture out where the sea of sand is always moving and the sky that is an Indian blue bowl upside down and where old gods make a mark when you come and another when you pass.

This pot pourri of desert articles contains something of it all, some history, some humor.

It is all bright, good country. Good for city sores. Good for smog burned lungs. Good for asphalt aches.

Approach it with care, as you would a new lover or a new religion, but approach it. Test it. Sample it. Maybe you'll agree with me then that after you've counted all of California's blessings and you've omitted the desert, you've omitted the salt. The spice. The thing that makes all the rest of it what it is. Mt. Whitney would just be the tallest peak in California, period, if it wasn't for the fact that behind Telescope Peak squatted Badwater. The ocean is two hours from the desert by freeway and that fact makes the ocean more exciting. Not the desert.

The desert is old and wise and comforting and destroying and friendly and cruel.

To me it is haven.

I go there when the blight is on the land and the locusts dim the sky and the fire burns on the hillside and the rocks slide and thunder down upon me. And the desert turns the blight into humor, the locusts into butterflies, the fire into sunset and the rockslide into distant hoofbeats of painted horses.

Come with me to the desert. Stay as long as I do or stay longer. Many have. They bless the day.

I FIRST SOME HISTORY—
THE MINES OF THE MOJAVE

It's hot here by summer and gas stations can be a long way apart. If you're seeking the more remote old ghost towns such as Panamint City and Modoc, do your exploring in a jeep. Good paved roads will take you to Randsburg, Darwin, Calico.

FOR ANYONE WHO EXPLORES the Mojave Desert, the best-known portion of California's desert country, it is helpful to know a little bit about the place. The following come-hither article will tell you some of the facts, some of the fictions. If you are going to make a career out of exploring the Mojave, there are acres of books on the subject, some you'll find listed in the bibliography in the back of this book. Mostly it was mining that made the desert what it is—or what it was, because it isn't today what it was then. Today it is air conditioning and piped water and cold beer. Yesterday it was walk and sweat and dream and hope and hope and hope.

There is a legend—and it is nothing more—that somewhere in the lonely, painted Panamint Range of the Mojave Desert, there is an elaborate treasure cave guarded by a balanced rock. Somewhere between Tin Mountain and Wingate Pass it is. Inside is the golden loot of the Paiutes—an anomaly, for the Paiutes were not a gold-grubbing tribe.

Historians may argue that this is a poor legend, and in spite of its persistence, call it fantasy.

But fantasy is woven into the rough cloth of the Mojave; it is as much a part of the region as the sand and the sun and the relentless spill of time. Trudged by Americans at least since 1844, the face of the Mojave has been changed only slightly,

3

One of the original Death Valley twenty mule team borax rigs, loaded, headed for Mojave.

and some of those changes have been patiently erased by the wash of wind and weather. Days wide and weeks deep, the Mojave is patently unreal to every visitor. Behind stone walls of outrageous colors it hides mossy gold. But when the gold is discovered it lies so deep, so deviously, that puzzled miners founder. There is a sense of fantasy in the mixture of geographies here; the secret ore bodies, the fossil footprints of prehistoric animals, the mark of early man, the burnish of desert pavement.

People who come to the Mojave come with a quest. The hurried men who first crossed here were seeking a route to the Pacific slope and gold. In the crossing some saw silver and many later poured back into the thirsty region searching for that silvery phantom. That special, secret silver has still not been found though shafts and tunnels dot the entire country.

To put a string around the Mojave Desert, stand somewhere on a high point of land east and south of Baldwin Lake in the San Bernardino Mountains. Push the line east to the Colorado River, north then along the border of California to a spot somewhere in Inyo County. West then, short of Owens Valley, and down along the Sierra Nevada, through the Piutes and Tehachapis to the San Gabriel and the San Bernardino Mountains.

Inside this rough rectangle is the Mojave Desert. Its commerces are many but always at the center is mining. Gold and silver and lead and tungsten; copper, too, and quicksilver; travertine and cement; gemstones and borax. The many mines here are old and the adits are choked with fallen timbers, yet gold and silver and lead and tungsten still wait for the bite of the pick and the rumble of the ore car.

Start then in 1844 with John C. Frémont, who put the name to the river in April that year after meeting natives from the Mojave territory. Frémont called the stream *Mohahve*. In 1860 a map by George H. Goddard labeled "the sink of the Mohave" as the area where the stream vanishes. Mohave Desert probably

Darwin, circa 1926. During its boom it had a population of around 5000.

won its name from the Wheeler Survey of 1875. After that geographers would argue the boundaries, but always the hard limits would elude them. The Mojave knows few roads, few towns, fewer houses than most of California.

Almost classic today is the account of the Jayhawkers and the others—California-bound gold seekers who left the Old Spanish Trail and struck due west. The *cul de sac* that finally stopped them was Death Valley. Only with difficulty did they extricate themselves from this waterless trap at the end of 1849.

During their escape from the Valley, somewhere in the Panamints, according to historian Harold O. Weight, the emigrants found native silver, nuggets of it, lying on top of the ground. One member of the group, a Captain Towne, whittled a bright piece into a gunsight to replace one that he had lost from his rifle. There was a momentary flurry of excitement. But the issue that day was salvation from the trackless, inhospitable region. If it was silver—and they agreed that it was—it would have to wait. They pushed on southwest. In six months the tale of the Death Valley crossing—and the silver gunsight—had percolated through the Mother Lode and the rest of California.

And in spite of the fact that the gold boom in the Mother Lode was going strong, three separate expeditions left the placers in 1850, looking for the Gunsight lode.

Soon it became the Lost Gunsight. From a small account it grew into a great legend that was repeated around a thousand campfires. Men, alleged to be members of the first Death Valley party, frequently acted as guides for many unsuccessful expeditions. Finally Dr. E. Darwin French, who ranched near Fort Tejon, took part in one of the searches, found nothing, but vowed to look again.

The expeditions multiplied, the Lost Gunsight became a ledge of silver, finally a mountain of silver; in the following years the trickle of prospectors looking for the lode became a flood.

7

*Interior of Randsburg saloon (and barber shop)
in the boom camp around 1900.*

French—with several others including Dennis Searles—made another foray into the badlands in 1860. This time French found silver, but it was miles away, in the Cosos. The party named places like Darwin Wash and Darwin Falls, the mountains and valley of Panamint, and probably labeled other landmarks.

The same year another party discovered antimony in the Wildrose country of the Panamints. And in time, because of the Lost Gunsight, there would be other discoveries of other minerals and metals.

The U.S. Navy took possession of the China Lake Naval Weapons Center in 1944. Within these 766,533 acres, known in the old days as "the Coso diggings," were 1,430 mining claims. Claims validated by the Navy showed that gold, silver, iron, lead, quicksilver, zinc, perlite, pumice and tungsten were still being mined in the area, all spawn of the Lost Gunsight.

From French's discovery of Coso new camps would come up. Out along the ridge of the Argus, Lookout Hill would blossom in 1875. Here George Hearst would fatten on a mineral feast and the Confidence, Lookout, Modoc, Keys and Hearst mines would burgeon. There would be boom towns at Modoc and Lookout.

Because of the silver mines and smelters in the Argus the ten great stone charcoal kilns were built up Wildrose Canyon in the Panamint Mountains. Charcoal was needed for the silver smelters and the Argus Range was bare. So the pinyon and other trees of the Panamints were felled and fed into the kilns. There was quite a camp at the kiln site at one time. You can make out the roughest of the foundation marks across the road from the beehive structures.

It was borax that brought reward to John Searles whose brother Dennis had been with the French party of 1860. John Searles probed the Gunsight country in 1862 and that year,

*Old Leadfield Hotel, scene of C. C. Julian's
boom town in Titus Canyon area of
Death Valley, has long since fallen down.
The heyday here for this spurious
lead boom was around 1925.*

crossing a vast dry lake southwest of the Panamints, idly picked up some crystals from the playa.

Ten years later, at Teel's Marsh in Nevada, Searles happened to witness the reclamation of borax from a dry lake. Searles remembered another dry lake southwest of the Panamints. The following year with his brother Dennis, he organized the San Bernardino Borax Mining Co., filed claim on the north end of the dry lake—it quickly became Searles Lake—and started digging. Trona stands here today.

It was impossible to keep Searles Lake a secret. Too many prospectors had scuffed the crystalline white stuff. Searles battled claim jumpers, San Francisco capitalists, the lack of water, summer heat and freighting problems to make the original 160-acre claim pay. What Searles started would, in time, pass on to Francis M. Smith and the Pacific Coast Borax Co.

In 1913 the mining operation became the American Trona Company—trona being a name for one of the chemicals in the thirty-square-mile lake deposit. The American Potash and Chemical Corporation succeeded the American Trona Company in 1926. Today the lake produces potash, soda ash, salt cake, borax, lithium, bromine and boric acid, and is one of the greatest chemical stockpiles in the country. Three billion, two hundred million tons of soluble salts await processing.

Another byproduct of the search for the Lost Gunsight was Cerro Gordo—Fat Hill. A silver-lead complex high above the rippling blue Owens Lake was found in 1865 by three Mexican prospectors according to historian W. A. Chalfant. The trio ran into Indians, and two were killed, but the third escaped after the Indians made him promise he'd not return to the rich slopes. But by 1868 the boom was on. The mines produced a rich silver-lead bullion, produced it faster than any camp in the history of the West.

It was the Gunsight search too, that pointed the way up

Water Wagon that served Randsburg in 1897.
Freighters hauled water 14 miles from
Indian Wells and sold it for $2 for a
50-gallon barrel.

Surprise Canyon, south of Wildrose and Telescope Peak in the Panamints, to a spot where R. C. Jacobs, W. L. Kennedy and R. Stewart found the silver in 1873 that gave birth to Panamint City, the roughest camp of them all.

With the miners came the badmen who held up the bullion wagons as they moved down the canyon. Even Wells Fargo, with some of the best shotgun riders in the West, turned down a Panamint City contract.

Still, Panamint City produced thousands of dollars in silver. Outlaws lived here, along with solid citizens, merchants, faro dealers, blacksmiths, saloon keepers, newspapermen and painted ladies. You can still recapture some of the mood from its ruined chimneys and stone foundations by driving up the rugged dirt road out of Ballarat. It's a drive for a jeep, really, but the reward is rich.

Back in the Coso country, the first mines at Darwin were located in November of 1874. By 1880 several mills and smelters were in operation and the camp had a population of 5,000. It was another tough town and while the surface ore could be reached easily the town flourished. Today it is just a slim shade away from being a ghost town. Tumbleweeds clot the streets. The road into Darwin from Keeler is a fine one and paved. Only no one goes that way any more. You tempt fate when you call any desert town a "ghost." If there is a single occupant left, he'll argue that the town will soon come back. Darwin folks are particularly proud people.

There are forgotten towns too. In 1906 Arthur Kunze, Frank McAllister and Hank Knight moved into Death Valley's Greenwater District onto some copper claims supposedly known for fifty years.

Greenwater, at its peak, had a population of about 5,000, with a post office, bank, two grocery stores and eight saloons.

Today at Greenwater there are only a few ruins. An old tin

*The Elite Theater in Randsburg,
   between 1895 and 1900.*

building stands at Greenwater Springs. Much more spooky, and dangerous, is Furnace about four miles north, where several deep, unmarked shafts perforate the desert floor. It is no place for wandering at night, nor by small children.

As Greenwater arose, so did Harrisburg and Skidoo over in the Panamints. It was gold, this time, not silver or copper. Skidoo earned its name because it was twenty-three miles to water and the expression "Twenty-three skidoo" was in vogue in 1906. Dirt roads and old workings mark the sites today. An old wooden hotel stood at Skidoo until a few years ago when vandals put the torch to it.

But the mining boom that made Death Valley famous was borax and that was in 1881 when Aaron Winters sold his borax claim to W. T. Coleman and Company for $20,000. Canny Isadore Daunet opened the Eagle Borax operation as fast as he could and shipped the first borax from Death Valley. After that came the Harmony Borax Works on the floor of the valley.

The famous twenty-mule teams hauled the borax out of Death Valley during those years after 1881. It was an incredible operation.

Part of the route from Harmony lay across the Devil's Golf Course, an area of ragged salt extrusions a yard high. This barrier was laboriously sledge-hammered flat by Chinese work-men—miles of it.

Down the Valley the route ran, past Bennett's Well, past the soon-abandoned Eagle Works, across the Devil's Golf Course, and on south to Wingate Wash, through the Panamints into the lonesome area south of Searles Lake, and then, over sandy patch and rocky outcropping, all the way to Mojave.

These hundred-foot-long spans of mules pulled two ore wagons and a water tank. The ore wagons, designed by J. W. S. Perry, mine superintendent, were built in Mojave for $900 each, had rear wheels seven feet high, front wheels five feet across.

15

Typical of the Mojave Desert's hand worked
mines of the early days is this view
of a Ludlow gold mine.

The steel tires were eight inches wide and one inch thick. The hubs were 18 inches in diameter and 22 inches long. The oak spokes were 5½ inches wide at the hub. The axle trees were solid steel bars, 3½ inches square, and deadly hot during those desert crossings. Empty, each wagon weighed 7,800 pounds. Loaded with borax it weighed 31,800 pounds. Two such wagons and a loaded tank—which held 1,200 gallons and weighed 9,600 pounds—made a total of 73,200 pounds or 36½ tons. That's what twenty-mule teams pulled out of Death Valley in those days. The trip from Harmony to Mojave took twenty days and the teams traveled fifteen to twenty miles a day. After 1915, Perry's grand towering wagons with the giant iron tires were replaced by the railroad. Death Valley was never the same.

One last mining boom in Death Valley is worthy of comment. In 1925 C. C. Julian, who would, in time, be branded a stock swindler and who would take his own life out in the Orient, developed Leadfield in Titus Canyon. There was lead here, true enough, but never in the quantities Julian sang about. He organized railroad excursions from Los Angeles to Beatty and motorcades from there into Leadfield where he poured champagne and served barbecued meat. In the east he circulated brochures showing Pacific steamers pulling up to the mouth of Titus Canyon to load Leadfield ore.

And shortly after the boom, came the bust. The road into Julian's Leadfield today is rough and only a few buildings still stand, a small bit of the fantasy of which the desert country is woven.

Calico had its day, too. A double-barreled boom. Horn silver was found in the Calico Hills in 1881 and a camp came up fast. Within a year 2,000 souls lived in the town; there was a main street, largely of tent buildings, but some of pink Calico adobe. Never a tough town, Calico lost only one citizen to gunplay in its first two years.

During those first two years borax was found near town. As silver went down, borax went up and Borate would be the name of the new Calico camp.

When the operation started at Borate, ore was freighted by mule team to the Daggett refinery twelve miles away. In 1894 the mule teams were replaced by "Old Dinah," a lumbering, coal burning, big-wheeled traction engine that could stomp out three miles an hour. Old Dinah, who stands in front of Furnace Creek Ranch in Death Valley now, was replaced by a railroad, the Borate and Daggett, one of the Mojave Desert's delightful short lines.

There were other short-lived railroads in the desert country. The Tonopah and Tidewater, which visited neither the tidewater nor Tonopah, ran north from Ludlow, seventy-odd miles east of Daggett, north to Baker and thence to Death Valley Junction. This was 1907. The Tonopah and Tidewater continued operation until 1940. In 1942 the government tore up the track for scrap steel.

The borax boom. Did it end when Ryan closed in 1928? Not at all. In 1913, while drilling for water on land he had homesteaded in Kern County, thirty miles east of Mojave, Dr. John Suckow struck a lode of colemanite. This was low-grade borax ore, but subsequent test holes revealed a large ore body of colemanite, crude borax, and finally a new mineral, first called razorite, then kernite. Production at Boron started about the time Ryan closed; the operation expanded greatly, and today almost pure borax is taken from the great open pit mine by modern methods. Boron is the Mojave Desert's biggest mine.

In 1895 three prospectors scouted south from Goler Gulch into the mountains that rose from Fremont Valley. In the washes they found gold, finally came to a ledge where they could chip out the bright metal. And thus the fantastic Yellow Aster mine of Randsburg was discovered—the Yellow Aster which would, in time, produce $20,000,000 for its owners.

Randsburg boomed. Tent and green board buildings went up all over the hillside. It was a rough town for a short time, then an active vigilante committee cooled off the hoodlums.

Atolia was born of a World War I tungsten strike. In 1918 Hampton Williams and Jack Nosser discovered silver at Red Mountain. The California Rand Silver Mine produced $20,000,-000 between 1920 and 1927.

With the exception of the Boron and Searles Lake operation, the Mojave Desert country is quieter now. There are real estate developments, and water has been found in deep wells.

The military is there. The Navy has the Inyokern wilderness and is looking for more. The Army's Fort Irwin hides the boom-camps of Copper City, Crackerjack, Garlic Springs, Denning Springs; Coolgardie sleeps nearby. There is Edwards Air Force Base.

Mines—gold, silver, cement, what you will—dot the region from Rosamond to the Colorado River.

Study a map of the Mojave today. There are still few main roads, little more than a score of places busy enough to earn a postoffice.

Days wide, weeks deep, the Mojave invites exploration in its tall, clear voice. By jeep they come now, looking perhaps, not for the Lost Gunsight, but for purple bottles at Greenwater, for square nails at Wildrose, for a scrap of paper relating to the Tonopah and Tidewater.

Still, in a manner of speaking, it is the Lost Gunsight that sends even today's explorer into the back country. For if it hadn't been for Captain Towne's idle whittling of a new gunsight of the soapy soft silver that winter's day in 1849, Coso and Lookout Hill, Randsburg and Old Harmony might never have risen.

The Lost Gunsight? Some historians claim this, too, is fantasy. Of such cobwebby stuff the sprawling Mojave Desert is fashioned.

II THROUGH EUREKA VALLEY INTO DEATH VALLEY

Avoid this in the summertime. Winter is fine. It's a long, lonesome road and you won't see much traffic. If this bothers you, go in a planned caravan of two cars or more. Stay on the bladed road. Don't mess around driving in the sand.

AS DEATH VALLEY HISTORY goes, there is a new entrance road into the National Monument, a dirt road, rough in places, that pierces an uncommon suburb of Death Valley and that is a pleasure to drive when the bite of heat is not on the land.

Once it was only a sandy track, running south from the lonesome desert of the Lida, Gold Point country and signed "one way road—down only." Now a fine graded road runs all the way from Big Pine in Owens Valley into the Monument near Ubehebe Crater and Scotty's Castle. It passes through a region of particular charm and unusual history and already it has become a favorite with many desert explorers.

The road, graded but unpaved from a point eighteen miles east of Big Pine, passes through Cowhorn Valley, skirts Saline Valley and the Waucoba country, pierces the volcanic Saline Range, bisects the wilderness of Eureka Valley, climbs and conquers the Last Chance Range, and drops down, finally, into the great northern expanse of Death Valley itself. It passes Sands Springs and gains pavement again on the road that leads out to Ubehebe Crater, six miles from Scotty's Castle.

Independence, county seat of Inyo County, is twenty-seven miles south of Big Pine. Try to arrange your time so you can stop here to visit, if only briefly, the Eastern California Museum.

The curator here will be happy to talk with you about the country you are going into. More, you'll find in the museum

20

relics of the area's past, including a boggling collection of historic photographs, some of them of vanished boom towns. You'll learn about the Museum's monthly field trip into the Owen's Valley country covering archeology, history and geology. You may wish to join the Museum Association in order to support their work and to receive the Museum's fascinating monthly newsletters.

At Big Pine a paved and signed road runs east toward Westgard Pass, the Ancient Bristlecone Pine Forest, Goldfield and Tonopah. Roughly two miles out of Big Pine, just as the narrow floor of the Owens Valley is crossed, we come to a junction where we turn right. Signs at this intersection read: "No accommodations or roadside resorts for the next seventy-eight miles," and, "Warning: do not attempt this route without ample supplies of water, gasoline and oil."

Heed these quiet warnings. For while the road you will travel

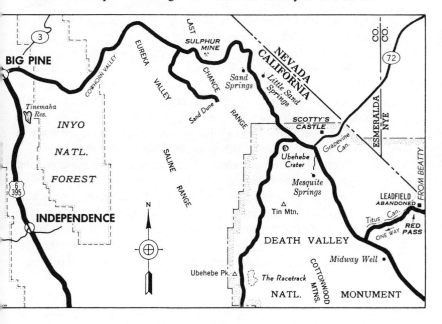

is usually a well-bladed road, wide enough for passing, easy enough for all passenger cars, uncomplicated enough for most flatland drivers, it does invade a remote area. Traffic on the road is not yet heavy. If you were to break down along the route you might have to wait for several hours before you received help. In addition to supplies for your car, include a good spare tire and tools to change it. Take warm clothing in the winter and cool spring, for it can become chilly here at night. Take along drinking water and food in the event you have to spend a night waiting for help. The Park Service suggests, further, that motorists using the road let some friend or relative know their plans, so that a search could be started in the event the traveler does not report by an appropriate time. The byway is not regularly patrolled by sheriff's deputies nor park personnel, but if you stay with your car some one will come along.

This is not alarmist talk. These are precautions wise drivers take when traveling any lonely road. We do not advise anyone to take this route in the summertime.

One last warning. If you are driving a passenger car, do not venture off the road with it. Park along the ample shoulder and hike out on either side of the byway if you wish, but leave the car beside the road on firm ground. There are frequent sandy spots where it is incredibly easy to get stuck.

As our road begins to climb a narrow canyon, look back at the Owens Valley and the Sierra Nevada backdrop.

There are many evidences of mining in the hills close at hand where strata are folded in unusual designs, inviting prospecting.

On up the streambed the road winds, the canyon pinching in. Beckoning the explorer, a large canyon opens off to the right, leading into the Inyo Mountains where timber can be seen on the higher peaks. And the byway climbs and climbs.

At a point roughly fourteen miles from our sideroad be-

*Rising to nearly 800 feet above the floor of
Eureka Valley is the great sand dune at the south
end of that desert depression. In the old days
explorers found arrowheads "by the bucketsfull"
around the giant dune.*

ginning, another junction is reached. One road bends away to the south into the Saline Valley. We take the road to the left, signed here and for the next many miles as the Loretta Mine Road.

We climb a brief summit, where stunted junipers stand, and ahead see our road crossing a small whitened dry lake.

This is Cowhorn Valley, a pleasant desert-mountain expanse. We climb toward another summit and there is more downgrade before Eureka Valley yawns. Along this approach the pavement ends, eighteen miles from the beginning of our sideroad. Joshua trees put in a brief appearance. As you drive, a great plume of dust ladders into the sky. A good idea when you meet someone along this dusty avenue is to crank up all your car's windows until the dust settles.

On over a steeper summit, then a down grade where the walls of the canyon squeeze in, and beyond is the first view-point with a panorama of Eureka Valley: at least twenty miles from north to south, here and there less than a quarter of that in width; sandy, flanked by strange desert peaks, flat, desolate.

The first formal exploration of this country took place in the summer of 1871 when a survey party under First Lieutenant George M. Wheeler, Corps of Engineers, U.S. Army, headed by Second Lieutenant D. A. Lyle, Second United States Artillery, struck west from Camp Independence into *terra incognita*.

Lyle's object was to determine if a route could be found "directly to the eastward over the sterile deserts and mountains intervening between the Amargosa and Owens rivers that was possible for a large train of men and animals." The exploration gave birth to tragedy and an unsolved mystery.

"Before I started," Lyle later told his superior, "I could get no information concerning the country to be traversed, and from every corner received discouraging accounts of the dangers at-

24

tending such a trip through a country entirely destitute of water, as far as known, after crossing the Inyo Range."

On July 21, 1871, regardless of the warning, the little band pushed off to the east, crossed the Owens River at Bend City, now vanished but even then deserted, and climbed the mountains via Mazourka Canyon. The first night out they camped at a site with water, grass and firewood.

Descending the Saline Valley side of the range (Lyle called it Salinas Valley) the party paused while a guide, C. F. R. Hahn, went ahead to look for water at the next planned campsite.

Hahn, according to historian W. A. Chalfant, was "one of the county's pioneers, discoverer of some of the mines of Cerro Gordo, an accomplished linguist and educated man as well as miner and mountaineer."

But Lyle later indicated that he had doubts. "From several previous interviews I had held with him in regard to this country, I had grave doubts as to whether he knew the country or not; these doubts were now painfully confirmed."

For Hahn did not return from his scouting.

The following morning, July 24, Hahn still missing, Lyle's party set out after him.

The trail climbed over the Saline Range, "a rocky, volcanic divide," that separated Saline Valley from Eureka Valley. Lyle's name for Eureka Valley was Termination Valley.

Crossing Eureka Valley became a nightmare for the explorers. They encountered "heavy sand-hills, over which the trail led, the mules sinking knee-deep at every step. The day was excessively hot. The wind, passing over the heated sand-hills, came in scorching gusts, rendering our sufferings intense and our thirst almost intolerable, while the incessant glare of the sun upon the white sand nearly blinded us and caused great pain in our eyes and heads after the first hours."

*The Big Pine to Death Valley road crosses
Eureka Valley and angles steeply up the west face
of the Last Chance Range.
Far to the south is the giant sand dune.*

By 5:00 P.M. Lyle's mules began to give out. Lyle scouted ahead into the Last Chance Range. He could see no avenue of advance, no sign of water, nothing hopeful, only the interminable desolation of the region.

The party pushed on, flanking the range now, turning into each side canyon as it was offered, hoping for a crossing, but without luck.

"Worn out and almost exhausted, we bivouacked on the heated, flinty surface to get a little rest; made coffee, our only fuel being some small bushes, and ate a little hard tack. We dared not eat more for fear of increasing our thirst.

"I concluded that [Hahn] had found the country worse than he anticipated, and had, no doubt, deserted us."

Lyle's shoes wore out; he put a pair of slippers on his lacerated feet. They camped in the inhospitable place for the night. The next morning the investigation of still another side canyon hinted that they had, at last, found a route through to the east. But the crew's elation was short-lived. This passage, too, was broken by steep waterfalls. Supplies had to be lowered over the cliffs by ropes. The stumbling mules barely made it to safety below.

But shortly afterwards a green spot was sighted on a nearby slope. A frantic scramble brought the party to the spring, which they christened "Last Chance Spring," and from which the range today takes its name.

Still Hahn was missing; nor did the party ever find him. They pushed ahead, finally rendezvoused with Wheeler's group in Death Valley.

Chalfant repeats the arguments offered in Owens Valley when Lyle's party returned: Lyle had made no effort to find Hahn. There were rumors that Hahn had failed to find water and had deserted, but many pointed the finger of guilt at Lyle. The temper of the Valley residents ran even higher when on his next

Death Valley Scotty's Castle in Grapevine Canyon
at the north end of Death Valley. The Castle
was started in 1926, finished in 1931.

A. M. Johnson, left; and Walter Scott; the
principal characters who built the Death Valley
Scotty legend. Chicago financier Johnson built
the Castle in Death Valley, Scotty made it live
in legend and history.

foray toward Death Valley Lyle lost another guide, another solid Owens Valley citizen, William Egan.

Chalfant writes: "While Wheeler and Lyle were both characterized as brutal and overbearing . . . the blame in both cases was Lyle's."

The misadventures of Lyle's party in Termination Valley and Last Chance Range gave the region a bad reputation. Shortly after the new byway was opened in 1962 a young motorist drove off the graded road into a sandy area near the great sand dune, the car became stuck and it was several days before he was rescued. Cached water in the area, placed there by wise desert explorers, helped save the motorist's life.

You will probably see some of this cached water if you turn off the graded Loretta Mine Road in the middle of the Eureka Valley and head south for ten miles to the giant dune. This road is also well graded, wide, perfectly safe as long as you stay on it. And because more than one car has been stuck in the soft, sandy spots off the road, the cached water has come in handy. Don't, as some senseless vandals have done, shoot up the gallon jugs of water partially buried in the sand. That water could save a life.

It is thirty-seven miles from the beginning of our byway to the sand dune turnoff.

The giant dune of southern Eureka Valley is probably close to 800 feet high, some say that it is five to eight miles around. It is a towering pile of wind-collected sand; white and fine and difficult to photograph. Old-timers in the Owens Valley will tell you that there was a time when you could collect arrowheads "by the bucketful" around the edge of the Dune. Today, alas, all the surface finds are gone, but thousands of chips remain, proof that the Indians did once fashion obsidian and jasper weapon points at this spot. But why here? It is hard to picture the giant dune as a favorite campground unless, in those arrow-making days, there was water or forage or food here.

It is perfectly safe to drive down to the dune. Turn around where you can see that other cars have turned around on the hard ground. Keep your car on the road. The mishaps have been caused by those who tried to drive across the sandy spots.

Back on the Loretta Mine Road we climb the west face of the Last Chance Range, past old mine tunnels and works, through narrow stretches of canyon.

Where the canyon widens, the road levels. Off to the left, just over five miles from the junction of the sand dune road, is a large sulphur mining operation. Our road descends, there is a brief upward pitch, and we are on the final descent into the upper elbow of Death Valley itself.

Our byway points down hill, to the south, past Sand Spring and Little Sand Spring, past shoulders of desert pavement where the boulders have been mysteriously cleared away (and where the old Indian trails are still plainly visible). Finally, seventy-one miles from that first warning sign, pavement is regained on the spur that runs out to Ubehebe Crater. Take this sideroad up to the one-way spur that skirts the big volcanic depression. The crater is 800 feet deep, a quarter of a mile across. There is a trail to the bottom, but a sign warns that you should first get ranger permission to make the hike. Volcanic cinders and "bombs" from the crater's eruption 3,000 years ago can be found as far as four miles away. Guidebook author Ruth Kirk claims that the place name comes from that of an old Indian woman who once lived in the area. Mrs. Kirk says the Indian name of the crater was Duhvee'tah Wah'sah—Duhveetah's Carrying Basket. Ubehebe Crater is the most spectacular of a half dozen volcanic pits there.

On to the west is the road again down into the Racetrack country. Again, check first with the local ranger before making this side trip. It is not recommended for the average city driver. It is very rough for the first ten miles, because it is merely scraped through the rocky material. Good desert drivers can make the trip with no trouble.

Seasonal rainstorms can wipe out any Death Valley road overnight. When in doubt, ask a ranger; even when you're not in doubt, ask one. Don't take chances.

It is the moving rocks that make the Racetrack such a point of interest. Boulders of all sizes apparently skate across the surface of the playa, leaving a track behind them. Scientists still argue whether it is wind, weather or the movement of the surface of the old dry lake that causes the rocks to move.

Most interesting site in this northern corner of the National Monument is Death Valley Scotty's Castle. You'll find it up Grapevine Canyon about three miles northeast from the road junction.

The legend of Water Scott, Death Valley Scotty, has been told a hundred ways. Among the facts about this colorful Valley figure are that he prospected here for many years and that he made his home in a small oasis near the site of the present Castle. Scotty's partner in later years was A. M. Johnson, Chicago financier who had been badly injured in a train wreck. Johnson's doctors told the millionaire that he needed a warm, dry climate, that without it they doubted if he would live to be forty. Johnson, as a result of a chance meeting, became friends with the former wild west show trick rider Scott, and Scott invited Johnson to Death Valley.

As a result of the friendship and the visit, the idea for the Castle was born. The structure was started about 1926, was finished in its present form in 1931 — and there are still several incompleted projects.

From the beginning it was called Scotty's Castle, although Johnson and his wife spent a good deal of time at the hideaway, which cost over $2,000,000.

The desert climate was good to Johnson. He was seventy-five

*Boulders of varying sizes with strange tracks
behind them in the surface of the dry lake are
a common sight at the Racetrack, a site reached
by a rough dirt road from the Scotty's Castle
area of northern Death Valley.*

when he died in 1948. Scotty died in 1954, aged eighty-one, and he and his dog, Windy, are buried on a hill behind the Castle.

For a while, at Johnson's request, the Castle was operated by the Gospel Foundation of California. Now it is part of the Monument, is staffed by Monument personnel and regularly scheduled tours are offered. In summer, when some of the lower Valley installations are closed, the Castle, at 3000 feet is open. It offers a snack bar, gasoline station, souvenir shop, parking area.

All tourists come away from the Castle tour impressed. They have seen the handsome imported furnishings. They may have sat in one of the down-filled leather chairs before the great fireplace in the main hall of the Castle, listening to the jasper-faced indoor waterfall tinkle moisture into the desert air. They have seen the great wooden beamed ceiling, the handsome wrought-iron work, the lavish use of hand-carved native redwood; the tile, the goatskin curtains, Spanish, Italian and handmade furniture.

In the music room an incredible organ, kept in working order, plays from a music roll. Neither the Johnsons nor Scotty could play this ornate instrument!

In a region packed with legends, the Scotty story is one of the most popular. No visitor to Death Valley should miss the Castle or the Castle tour. There is current talk that the Park Service may take over the Castle.

South from Scotty's Castle, on the main Valley road, the Grapevine ranger station is passed, and off to the right is the campground at Mesquite Spring.

Travel this highway early in the morning or at twilight when the shadows are long. The sun then picks out startling highlights in the Cottonwood Mountains and Tin Mountains to the west; and the Grapevine Mountains to the east.

Through a slot in the Grapevines runs Titus Canyon. Entrance to this one-way road lies east, out along the road to Beatty. The sideroad, on the left, almost at Beatty, is plainly marked. The dirt road leads back, thirteen and a half miles, through foothill country, then up abruptly and steeply to Red Pass, and down into abandoned Leadfield, site of a stock speculation promotion in 1926. The lead in Leadfield was low grade, useless stuff, and the only person who made anything from it was promoter C. C. Julian.

Below the ghost of Leadfield is Klare Spring, with some Indian petroglyphs; and then the road enters narrow-walled Titus Canyon. For more than two miles you pass through this twisting canyon. In places, passengers can reach out of your car and touch either wall of the canyon. Above, the cliff lifts to 500 feet. There are mud scars fifteen feet high on the walls to show high water marks during summer flash floods.

Again, it is possible that recent storms have closed this road temporarily. Check with the local rangers.

Back on the main Valley road is Midway Well, another campground, and then comes the sideroad to the sand dunes. South are the better-known attractions of the Valley: Furnace Creek, Badwater and the stunning exhibits at the Visitor's Center.

Death Valley via Big Pine is only a whisper now, but it is a byway byword that will grow in volume as more travelers find this handsome route.

On a cool spring day, Eureka Valley and the Last Chance Range lie tamed beneath skies of incredible blue. But by summer, more experienced desert travelers than Lt. Lyle might have misgivings about such a crossing.

III REMEMBER WICKED, WICKED PANAMINT CITY?

This is a cool weather trip. The rough road areas should be asked about first, some of them are only jeep tracks at best. Take breakdown emergencies, it's rugged country—but such historic and wonderful land.

PERHAPS FROM A LOW flying airplane you could trace the old pack mule and wagon route from the Modoc Mine, up in the rim country of the Argus Mountains—in southern Inyo County, across the waist of the Panamint Valley to the charcoal kilns in lofty Wildrose Canyon.

But as far as the spectator on the ground is concerned, that road has vanished. Yet considering the few short years that it existed, the route from Modoc to Wildrose was perhaps the most heavily traveled road in the Panamint Valley until modern times.

It happened in the 1860's. The years-long search for the fabled Lost Gunsight lode had resulted in the discovery of many rich or almost rich mining properties in the desolate country west of Death Valley. The Modoc, in the Lookout district of the Argus Range and owned by George Hearst, was one of these. It was a silver deposit and silver ore processing called for smelting. But there were no trees on the Argus; no trees, no charcoal for the smelter. Hearst ordered a team of Swiss stonemasons into the purple Panamints to the east across the Panamint Valley. Here they built a row of thirty-foot beehive kilns. The diminutive piñon, mountain mahogany, bristlecone and limber pine of the Panamints were fed into the charcoal kilns and the charcoal was hauled by pack mules and wagons across the Panamint Valley to the Lookout smelters.

Today the once-sinful boom towns of Modoc, Lookout and

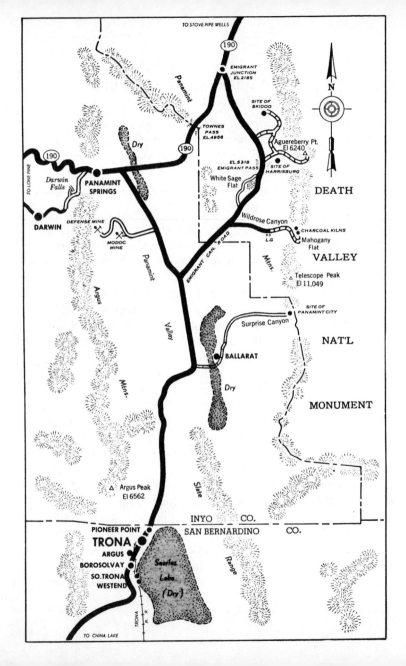

Defense, and the kiln camp of Wildrose have vanished. But the kilns still stand and these and other relics of those golden days of desert boom make a trip to the Panamint country a fascinating excursion into gaudy history.

The land here is fair, an immense pastel-hued wilderness where roads are few and the air is clean. An extra dividend for the byway explorer.

This corner of desert country is reached via U.S. Highways 14 or 395 from the Southland. From these highways a good road runs east past the China Lake naval base, Ridgecrest, on east along the southern boundary of the Naval Weapons Center through Salt Wells Valley into the Trona complex.

This collection of communities derives its existence in a relativelly isolated location from the rich chemical deposits laid down in ancient Searles Lake. There are six separate communities here: Pioneer Point, Trona, Argus, Borosolvay, South Trona and Westend. Their combined populations total almost 5,000. Largest of the lot is Trona, the home base for the American Potash and Chemical Corporation which employs 900.

First sighted in 1849 by emigrants fighting their way out of the Death Valley trap, Searles Lakes was found again by prospector John Searles in 1862. Here he saw crystals of borax and later discovered their value. In 1874 Searles established the San Bernardino Mining Company, pioneered in the harvesting of surface borax, then sold the operation in 1896. The site was quiet then until 1913 when the mining operation was reorganized as the American Trona Company—trona being a name for one of the chemicals in the thirty-square-mile crystalline lake deposit. The American Potash and Chemical Corporation succeeded the American Trona Company in 1926. The lake gives up potash, soda ash, salt cake, borax, lithium, bromine and boric acid.

Beyond, on the good paved road that leads north, is forty-five-mile-long Panamint Valley, picturesque smaller sister of

Aerial view of the giant plant at Trona. Operation treats chemicals obtained from nearby Searles Lake.

Death Valley which lies just east over the Panamint Range to the east.

According to historian W. A. Chalfant, among the first white men to see the valley were the Jayhawkers under Captain Ed Doty. Fighting their way west out of Death Valley on foot during that awful winter of 1849, the Jayhawkers climbed the Panamint Range west of Emigrant Pass, hoping to see the valley of Los Angeles when they reached the summit. Instead they saw and descended into Panamint Valley, and down this depression they stumbled past Searles Lake into the Mojave Desert and eventual safety.

Here history grows dim. One fact, however, is quite clear. When white men returned to the desert area, it was the Lost Gunsight lode that brought them back.

In the straggling group of Death Valley emigrants with the Jayhawkers were Captain Towne and Jim Martin, members of a group called the Georgia and Mississippi Group or the Bugsmashers. In the area of White Sage Flat in the Panamints, Towne—history spells his name in many ways but Towne at least has received geographic recognition—turned up with a soft piece of bright silver from which he whittled a new gunsight for his damaged rifle. Later, it might have been that same day or the next, Towne and Martin picked up more specimens of the silver ore. They told their comrades of the richness of the area where the ore was found.

But at that time their chief interest was getting to civilization and the gold fields of the Mother Lode. The following year the first of the Lost Gunsight lode seekers were back in the Panamints. And while the mesa that was sprinkled with the silver ore was never found, the Panamint country was opened up as a result of the searching.

The Coso, Argus and Slate Ranges were prospected. The

Panamint Range—which drew its name from local Indians—was explored. Telescope Peak was climbed.

Darwin French sent expeditions into the wilderness and left behind him a camp, a wash, a canyon and a waterfall that still bear his name.

Coso boomed in 1860. The Telescope mining district was born and after it came the Argus district. The Lookout area came up and the charcoal kilns were built in Wildrose Canyon for the Modoc smelters. In 1873 the discovery of copper-silver glance led the rush to Panamint City, up steep Surprise Canyon. After that came Harrisburg and Skidoo.

When Skidoo died the country quieted down and slow growing desert chaparral inched up in the pack mule and wagon roads; the inquisitive fingers of wind picked to pieces the skeletons of the buildings left behind when boom turned to bust.

Roughly thirty miles north of Trona a dirt track departs from the ribbon of blacktop that runs the length of Panamint Valley and hurries east toward the dark, textured Panamint Mountains.

First a speck at the foot of the enormous wall of mountains, then, as you draw closer, a ragged cluster of buildings and ruins, is old Ballarat.

Once this was a main supply station for the mines in the Panamint country. There was a post office here in 1898. But today there are mostly ruins.

From Ballarat a dirt road leads north, then east up the giant alluvial fan into Surprise Canyon and on to Panamint City.

This is no drive for the average passenger car or average city driver. It is steep, rough, narrow, sometimes muddy—a spring empties its water down the track in places. The road can ruin a modern car and give a flatland driver the shudders. Leave the drive to jeeps, pickups and Volkswagens—seemingly the only passenger cars that can make the nine-mile climb without disaster. For those who can make the trip, the sight of the ruins of

Panamint City—a wicked town that boomed, lasted roughly two years and was then scoured away by a mountain cloudburst—is an exciting reward. Foundations and a great red brick chimney are about all that remain here. But ghosts are everywhere among the 6,640-foot-high ruins.

Thirty miles north of Trona there is a fork in the paved road. The left-hand branch leads on through the Panamint Valley to Panamint Springs and Townes Pass. We take the right-hand branch, the Emigrant Canyon Road, and follow it up the gentle climb into Wildrose Canyon, past the Death Valley National Monument entrance marker and the small resort of Wildrose Station, to another fork in the road. Here again we take the right-hand branch and it leads past a ranger station and up the hill toward the storied charcoal kilns.

The road is paved for about half of the seven-mile climb to the kilns. The dirt portion is deceptively steep. Shift into lower gear here or your car may be boiling when you arrive at the landmark.

Ten great conical kilns are standing. Weather has inflicted little harm. You can walk inside the great sooty structures. Behind the row is a smaller lime kiln.

On the west side of the road stood the old kiln camp and debris from this vanished community marks the site.

The dirt road continues on past the kilns for more than a mile past Thorndike's Park Service campground—there is water here—on up a steep pitch and narrow road to Mahogany Flat. From the parking area a brief spur road runs north along the top of the 8,133-foot-high flatland to several attractive picnic sites. Without much difficulty it is possible to find a clearing in the forest and to look down from this summit into the great depression of Death Valley.

A new road, built in 1959 but permanently closed to the public, leads up the hill from Mahogany Flat toward 11,049-foot

41

*The picturesque charcoal kilns in Wildrose
Canyon up on the side of the Panamint Mountains.
Kilns were built to make charcoal for smelters
across Panamint Valley in mines in the
Coso and Argus Mountains.*

*Mining operations have been carried on in
recent years at the site of old Harrisburg.*

Telescope Peak. The road extends as far as Rogers Peak, elevation 9,994 feet, where a radio repeater station is now located. A foot trail reaches back from Rogers Peak to Telescope Peak, a spire that dominates the entire desert region.

On the drive down Wildrose Canyon keep your eyes on the right side of the canyon below the kilns for the scar where the historic pipeline was built. It ran twenty-three miles from Telescope Peak to Skidoo carrying water for that more isolated community. The pipeline is gone but its route is faintly discernable.

Back on the Emigrant Canyon Road we turn right and head north.

To the left here is White Sage Flat where Captain Towne and Jim Martin found the silver ore that became the Lost Gunsight lode. There is a rough jeep road leading down to the Flat.

Ten miles past the Wildrose Canyon road is the signed turn-off for the Harrisburg-Aguereberry Point dirt road.

There is little left at the site of Harrisburg, a flat where prospector Shorty Harris made a rich find in 1906. Harrisburg was largely a tent city and, while debris and a couple of open shafts mark the spot, only a single weathered, more recent building stands here now.

Five miles beyond Harrisburg Flat is Aguereberry Point, a spectacular overlook into Death Valley. This site is named after Pete Aguereberry, another Death Valley character of yesterday. His name is spelled variously by the many histories of the area and era.

Back at the site of Harrisburg, a good dirt road winds north for 3.6 miles and connects with another dirt road running in from Emigrant Canyon Road. This new dirt road leads back to the site of Skidoo.

This dirt road is meaner than anything we have yet encountered on this byway—except the road up Surprise Canyon. It is not steep, but it is rough and studded with large rocks throughout

Part way up Surprise Canyon—and about as far as a normal passenger car can go—is this green and watery site: Chris Wicht's Camp. Spring runs year around.

its five-mile run back to the camp founded in 1906 by Harry Ramsey, John Thompson and Bob Montgomery. The name comes from that twenty-three-mile-long pipeline that carried water to the community, and a smart saying of the day: "Twenty-three skidoo." At least this is one of the unsubstantiated legends about the town's uncommon name.

The historic marker designating the site of Skidoo stands on a flatland. This was the rowdier part of the old camp. There is a boothill here, for Skidoo was a wild one. When founder Ramsey was stabbed and killed—according to legend—the outraged citizens caught a suspect and promptly hanged him. After they cut down the body someone remembered they had not taken a photograph of the act. So they hanged the man again, and this time took a picture. After that Skidoo was known as "the town where they had the hanging." The boothill, incidentally, has been shockingly vandalized.

Beyond the flat, less than a mile, stood the more substantial part of old Skidoo on a hill. A couple of buildings remain, but the famous old mine administration building, with its broad veranda and sweeping view of Death Valley, burned down in 1961.

Sightseeing on foot is fascinating. There are tunnels to peer into—but stay out of them. The Million Dollar Stope is here, a great hollowed-out section of mountain where a fabulous quantity of rich ore was extracted. Warning: there are also open shafts in the ground that are unfenced. Keep small active children carefully in hand. Some of the shafts are very deep.

Back now, down this rough and dusty road to Emigrant Canyon Road pavement, then on toward Death Valley, to Emigrant Junction, then double back, to the west, up and over steep Townes Pass. Heed the signs warning of steep grades.

At the bottom of the hill this byway—it is State Highway 190 —crosses a great dry lake. In the buttes to the north, near the distant sand dunes, fossils have been found. On west, the highway passes Panamint Springs resort and about a mile farther comes to an unmarked dirt road turning off to the south.

This road is rough, but neither steep nor dangerous. It goes back about three miles to Darwin Falls.

It is unfortunate that so many careless people have left litter at the parking area here, but this is the fate of many desert sites. Hike up the canyon for about a quarter of a mile to the falls. The hike is rugged, but the sight of the twenty-foot falls, the ferns and the willows growing in the desert, makes it more than worthwhile. One of the mysteries of the desert country, a constant flowing spring, provides water for the falls and the ferny oasis.

If you continue on this very bad dirt road to the west you will emerge at Darwin, but the route is not recommended for passenger cars.

Instead, return on Highway 190, turn right on the Panamint Valley byway about three miles east of Panamint Springs, and as you drive south back toward Ballarat and Trona study the rim of the Argus Mountains to the west for the roads and scars of the mines of Modoc, Minietta, Lookout and Defense. Even without binoculars it is possible to see some of the historic diggings.

Study the barren, boulder-studded valley and try, if you can, to spot the place where the pack mules and wagons crossed from Modoc to the kilns of Wildrose.

Study, too, the tortured and eroded hills to the east. People the picture with the Jayhawkers, the Bug-smashers, the searchers for the Lost Gunsight, prospectors Shorty Harris and Johnny Ramsey.

Pause north of Ballarat and study that awesome alluvial fan that spreads out from the tight-lipped mouth of Surprise Canyon and visualize the traffic that once traveled that narrow thoroughfare when Panamint City boomed at the top.

There are many who say that Panamint Valley is the most ghost-ridden plot of real estate in all the desert country, that these presences can be felt, especially late on winter afternoons when the sun inches down behind the Argus and Coso ranges and a chill wind walks the great dry lake.

Even the most insensitive will admit there is a feel about the place, but these will probably blame the mood on the emptiness, the size, the setting of the Panamint country.

All ghost stories discounted, Panamint country does have moods, many of them depending on the time of the day and the weather. This time of the year most of these moods are exhilarating. If you catch the place in a bad mood, blame it on wind or clouds or shadows.

If there are ghosts here, they are those of the adventurers who helped to build the West. They mean you no harm.

The ruined smelter chimney at old Panamint City.
Vandals have torn down much of the
old structure.

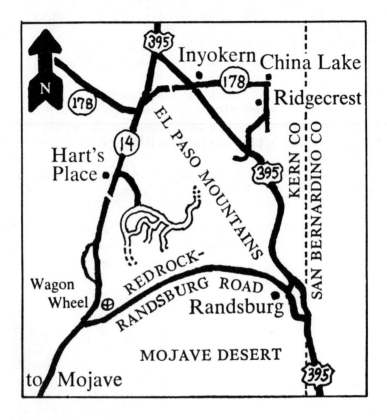

IV A RING AROUND THE EL PASO MOUNTAINS

*Can be hot by summer. Circle can be completed
in a day but with a jeep or truck the exploration
possibilities are unlimited. Take normal precautions.*

IN AN ARID REGION largely overlooked by historians, there is one
shadowy desert range that stands apart. The El Paso Mountains
of northeast Kern County are represented in more than a dozen
regional volumes, and the general theme of the writing is the
same. This is a strange, tortured, moody, wind-bitten, sun-
slashed, miner-clawed land. For those who would brave the
simple dangers, there are good roads that first skirt the range,
then, taking courage, probe back into the mysteries. It has
always been good hunting.

Whenever the press of city living wounds the muscles and the
mind, this is the kind of country that works like medicine. The
sky is painted with the longest handled brush. The mountains in
this part of the Mojave stand in geometric disarray, touching
each point of the compass and wearing the purple of distance.
When you look close at hand they reveal more intimate colors.
Roads that measure the range taper and vanish straight-line
ahead, seeking out some elusive horizon that always seems to
hide in the next county.

The El Pasos, if you read the books, have always known the
suffering of gold mining. Hidden here are the secret places where
the "old people" made primitive magic. There are canyons
where the painted rocks hang in folds and gather like curtain
cloth. The El Pasos have logged the heartbeat of stamp mills, the
scrape of burrowers, the light-footed pacing of bighorn sheep.

For this desert adventure we will start at the old Wagon Wheel

*The folds of sculptured rock hang in
disarray in Red Rock Canyon area.
Region once knew gold mining boom.*

restaurant on State Highway 14 at the junction of the Redrock-Randsburg road. (The restaurant may be closed; it has known random periods of closure in years past.) You will be making a crooked circle trip to see the El Pasos on this byway. You will return to the Wagon Wheel later in the day.

Just north of the Wagon Wheel on State Highway 14 you enter a region of the desert country known as Red Rock Canyon. It is more. It is a sprawling area that knows sculptured rock formations, bright colors, history.

Historian-museum curator Richard C. Bailey wrote one of the best accounts of the Red Rock mystery in the 1964 edition of the Los Angeles Corral's *Westerners Brand Book,* volume number 11. It is a book that is almost impossible to find in book shops today but it contains some unique desert material. Bailey's article on Red Rock Canyon is detailed and descriptive.

The old place names alone in Red Rock Canyon will give you a sense of the place. Maybe they were made up by a yesterday cartographer out of whimsy, maybe not. But reckon with the Towers of Silence, Tombstone Ruins, Magic Silent City, Royal Gate, Liberty Dome, Griffin Pool, Buried City, Temple of the Sun, Lava Whirlpool, Red Rooster Point, Shrine of Solitude.

There was a gold mining flurry here in 1893. Miners then indicated that there was evidence that some placering had taken place in the area as early as 1860. Records show that $16 million in placer gold was taken from the Red Rock area during the 1890s.

There are older roads in the area but today four-laned State Highway 14 passes through the main canyon channel. There are impressive formations on either side of the highway, places to turn off and park, lanes that lead deep into the region where campers, trailers, motorcycles, jeepers, hikers and photographers can explore. Partway through the canyon is the paved side road to the west, a stretch of the old road that leads past the site of

*Tumbleweeds are creeping up on this outpost
on the Mojave: the old and abandoned
general store at Cantil.*

vanished Ricardo—only a pile of rubble was left here when we last passed—and entrance spots to more trailer and motorcycle areas in the northwest Red Rock area.

Photographers go slightly wild in Red Rock Canyon. There are hues here to tease the color film addict, and there are shapes and shadows to beguile the black-and-white artist. Walking the region only discloses more and more of the ruined cities, the buried temple formations. And in spite of dirt tracks there is no route for jeepsters from east Red Rock to Last Chance Canyon deeper in the El Pasos. If you do follow these tracks you'll find only a dead end or a loop back before you have gone many miles.

But from currently closed Hart's Place, seven or more miles to the north on State Highway 14, you will find an unpaved avenue leading deep into the mystic El Pasos.

This road is unnamed, is dusty and washboarded in most places, is wide enough to pass an oncoming car, can be driven by modern passenger cars for a way. It takes off directly east of Hart's Place and on the map runs all the way to Holly Camp, meets the Last Chance Canyon road, explores Copper Basin, touches Burro Schmidt's Tunnel, runs on in diminishing proportions, to junction with the Mesquite Canyon road, and then points north toward Inyokern. There are side road offerings off this El Paso Mountains network as well.

But in all honesty, this is not all passenger car country, no matter how beguiling the sites offered. Last Chance and Mesquite Canyon should not be essayed by passenger cars at all. The Hart's Place road is the *only* safe passenger car entrance into the El Pasos. Drive it only as far as you feel comfortable. This might be the top of the hill up from Hart's Place. It might be Holly Camp. If the road is packed solid and the sandy spots do not grab at your tires, you might be able to go all the way to Copper Basin and Burro Schmidt's Tunnel.

We got to the top of the hill east of Hart's and were discour-

*Like so many shops in Randsburg, this barber
shop-art gallery is usually locked. Randsburg
has lost much of its old glitter.*

aged by the way the jeeps before us had churned up the sandy pockets in the road ahead. This is a fantastically popular jeep and motorcycle country. You'll find it used by rockhounds, prospectors, fossil hunters (there is a piece of a petrified forest off the Last Chance Canyon avenue).

But even from the rise we were able to look back into the heart of the El Pasos and dream a little.

Back in Copper Basin there is a ruined movie set, which has lost much of its earlier grandeur but still is fun to explore.

Burro Schmidt's Tunnel is a monument to the determination of a single man who wanted to drive a bore through a mountain. You can rent a lantern and walk through the half mile tunnel and look out at Fremont Valley and the Rand Mountains to the south. It was completed in 1938. Schmidt is dead now, but Mrs. Tonie Seger operates the site. Even Ripley wrote about the curiosity of the human mole who dug a 2,000-foot tunnel and touched not one speck of pay ore in the passage.

Farther back is Block Mountain. On the summit are some strange pictographs and rock circles. Richard Bailey, in *Explorations in Kern,* describes a winter hiking trip to the strange ceremonial Indian site.

But let us continue north on State Highway 14 from Hart's Place. The next road junction is with State Highway 178, the Walker Pass road, coming in from the west. Back here, near the junction, is the site of vanished Coyote Holes, later called Freeman Junction, where Tiburcio Vasquez once robbed the stage station—that was in 1874, history here has an elder flavor. Read E. I. Edwards' *Freeman's, a Stage Stop on the Mojave* for details of the raid.

North now to the Inyokern-China Lake-Ridgecrest turnoff, an extension of State Highway 178 to the east.

Within the Naval Weapons Center base at China Lake is the small but fascinating Maturango Museum. It is only open from

Wind, weather, time have taken their toll of this windmill and residence in faded Garlock.

2 to 5 P.M. on Saturday and Sunday afternoons. (It is open to special groups by prior arrangement.)

You are allowed into the base, and there is a parking place at the museum. Inside you'll find displays on the Indians of the area, their artwork, their pictographs and petroglyphs, which can be found in the Weapons Center range. There is a display of antique bottles found in the desert around China Lake. Desert fish are exhibited. There are insect, reptile, bird, animal, plant, butterfly displays. Minerals are important in the area and are also on exhibit. Relics from desert ghost towns are there too.

The historical museum is crowded into a small room and a narrow hall. Getting more space and attention is an adjoining museum devoted to the Navy weaponry developed at China Lake.

The museum offers field trips to members, a publishing program (the interesting *Indian Wells Valley Handbook* is now in its fourth printing and is a sound investment for an area explorer). From time to time the museum leads expeditions back to the Petroglyph Canyons area. All history, desert and Indian buffs should arrange to attend one of these outings. Few places in California contain such a concentration of the ancient rock writing of the aboriginal people—the "old people"—of the Mojave.

In 1969 a new publication came out of the Museum here about the rock writing of the "old people." This paperback is called *Rock Drawings of the Coso Range* and was written by Campbell Grant, James W. Baird and J. Kenneth Pringle. It is liberally illustrated, is not designed only for the expert, and contains a useful bibliography of other things you can read about the strange Coso area.

South of Ridgecrest, China Lake Road runs into U.S. Highway 395 and offers a route around the other side, the east side of the El Pasos.

*Indian lore of the area draws the most visitors
to the Maturango Museum at China Lake.*

Old mines, tailing piles, headframes can be found in this region. There is the track of the seldom-used Southern Pacific Railroad line from Mojave to Owens Lake. There is the spur to Trona and Searles Lake. You'll usually find chemical cars parked on the sidings here.

Then into the pass between the El Pasos and the Summit Range, down into the uppermost arm of Fremont Valley and ahead, sparkling on the hillside, is the glitter of Randsburg.

The glitter is mostly mirage. There is little real glitter at Randsburg today. Most of the stores are shuttered. A couple of bars, a grocery store, the post office are open on a regular basis. Purington's Desert Shop is still open on weekends. Here a pair of delightful desert folks, the A. E. Puringtons, sell antique bottles with an honest personal discovery story to go with each bottle sale. These folks, of a growing fraternity, spend their weekdays prowling the lonely reaches of the desert looking for bottles and their luck has been phenomenal.

There is a small but interesting county museum in Randsburg, open only on weekends. There are a couple of old buildings, which are fun to photograph, but there is a general air of decay in the place, and it is a pity. Randsburg had such a gala and illustrious past, it is a pity that more of the grand life doesn't show. There is not a single great old house left.

When the Yellow Aster Mine first came up, there was no mill at Randsburg. The ore was freighted down the hill, across the desert to Cow Wells where the big stamps were located. Later Cow Wells would be known as Garlock and the mill would shut down and this desert camp would almost completely ghost.

From Garlock the Red Rock-to-Randsburg road runs west, past the entrance to Last Chance Canyon (don't try it in your new Camaro), past the entrance to Saltdale on the other side of the road. That patch of white out there is Koehn Dry Lake, and the patch of green is alfalfa where farmers have irrigated from the vast underground pool of fresh water, which made this corner of Fremont Valley flourish.

At Cantil you'll find the old general store empty, windows gone, the weathered ties that make up the walls silvering in the winter sun. Near Cantil are lush fields of alfalfa, irrigated with a lavish hand.

On then, around a corner and north and you are back at the Wagon Wheel restaurant. Maybe it will be open.

The bulk of the El Pasos sits to the northeast now. You can count the canyons and almost canyons. The movement in the brush are jackrabbits. They hide all along the Red Rock-Randsburg road.

Desert regulars have asked me, "What is it all about—the El Pasos? I find myself going back there again and again, to nibble at the edges and to feast on the range itself. What is it that attracts?"

It is a difficult question to answer. First you must concede that the questioner is a desert fan or he wouldn't be beguiled by the country at all. Then you know he must have done his homework or he wouldn't know of the secrets that are hidden here.

Beyond that it is the contrast and the color and the legends and the history that make up the magnet.

You'll want one day to walk Burro Schmidt's Tunnel, even if you don't make it this time.

You'd like to climb Black Mountain to see those rock circles.

You'd enjoy finding a piece of petrified palm off Last Chance Canyon.

And around the edges. You'll take pictures at Red Rock. You'll covet the desert bottles at Maturango Museum. You'll talk long to A. E. Purington.

In a day you can touch most of this country, touch it, if not experience it all deeply. It is about 80 miles around it all, from Wagon Wheel to Wagon Wheel. If you have a jeep or pickup, your adventure will be entirely different, you'll probably spend the day on the interior of the range.

If you spot a photographer taking a hundred pictures of the folds and gathers of stone in Red Rock Canyon, both in color and black and white, chances are that will be me.

I never tire of the place. I've yet to find the Towers of Silence, the Tombstone Ruins, the Magic Silent City and some of the other highlights there.

But I keep looking, year after desert year.

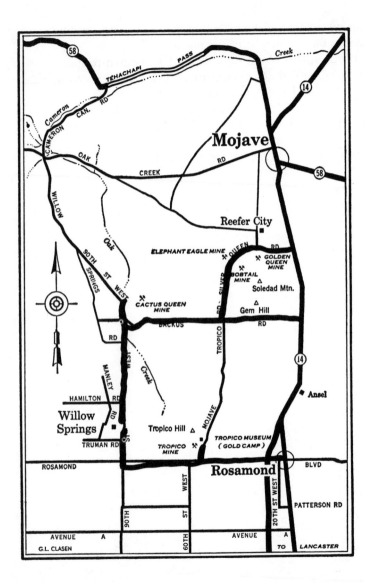

V WHERE EZRA HAMILTON
STRUCK IT RICH

It's generally more fun to visit this area when it
is cool; the Mine and the Gold Camp are usually
shut down by deep summer. But rockhounds haunt the
area throughout the year.

THERE WAS A TIME, and within the memory of men still living, when there were antelope in the Antelope Valley. From the Tehachapis far out into the desert they roamed and when people tried to count them they tallied more than 7,000 in a day's spotting and gave up. The antelope, they agreed, would be here forever.

They had not considered the antelope's reaction to the railroad that put a path of steel across their grazing ground in 1876. The antelope would not cross the tracks. They piled up against the ribbons of steel and starved to death there rather than cross the few feet. And then, in the 1880's, a nightmare storm visited the Valley. Snow stood in deep drifts and the antelope froze or starved and the coyotes grew fat that winter.

As late as 1910 there were still a few antelope left in the Valley; fences and settlers put an end to them; today youngsters don't understand such a place name. Call it Joshua Tree Valley, they say; or even Gold Valley. For surely much gold was taken from the burned hills here. The buttery yellow metal was produced in quantities into the millions, and how it was found in the beginning concerns a small and minor mystery that still has not been solved.

Why did Ezra Hamilton pan the fire clay that was shipped to him from the Antelope Valley?

Fire clay was discovered on Crandall Hill, near Rosamond,

63

Entrance to the Burton Tropico Mine—the tour takes you back along the surface level. The mine is safe and well lighted but you can peer down into deep and spooky shafts.

in the 1870's. It was shipped to Ezra Hamilton's East Side Pottery plant in Los Angeles where "fire brick, hollow brick, drain tile, sewer and water pipe, jugs, stoneware, terra cotta flower pots and ornamental vase works of all kinds" were made.

In 1882 Hamilton bought Crandall Hill and its clay deposits, changed the name of the place to Hamilton Hill and stepped up production.

By 1894 a kind of recession had hit Los Angeles' pottery and brick business. Historians record that it was during this time that Hamilton idly panned some of the fire clay and found gold. As a result of that idle panning, Hamilton started looking for gold.

It took time, and Hamilton, complaining all the while of being "sick and disabled," found the hillside lode in 1896 and called the claim the Lida Mine.

According to Glen Settle, Antelope Valley historian, "jewelry rock" came out of the stopes here. "He had assays that ran as high as $96,000 per ton. In 1904 his gold was exhibited at the World's Fair in St. Louis and was the hit of the mineral show." Settle adds that Hamilton never got back his ore samples from the Fair.

Almost overnight Hamilton was rich. He admits to making $200,000 from the mine and may have made as much as $750,000. Impressed with the healthful qualities of the area, he bought in 1900 the historic stage station of Willow Springs for $3,500—the springs and 160 acres of land. And he spent $40,000 improving the property.

Willow Springs became a show place. There was a hotel, cottages, a bathhouse, a public hall, a blacksmith shop, stables. Most of these were uniformly designed, built of local rock. Many still stand and, aside from some earthquake damage, are sound.

By 1906 Hamilton was firmly committed to the Willow

*Aerial view of Burton's Tropico Mine and
Gold Camp near Rosamond.*

Springs experiment. He regarded it as a health resort. Tuberculosis victims came with only weeks to live and lived for decades —this is the kind of story they tell about old Willow Springs. Hamilton invented a machine that would lay continuous cement pipe and he used the machine and pipe at the Springs. He experimented with silk worms and mulberry trees; he planted orchards and vines. He claimed his grapes were the sweetest in the West and his wine the tastiest.

In 1908 Hamilton sold the Lida Mine and other claims on Hamilton Hill to the Antelope Valley Milling Co. The following year they, in turn, sold the property to the Tropico Mining and Milling Co. The principals came from the old town of Tropico near Glendale, and they brought their home town name with them. It was the Tropico Mine, now, and Tropico Hill.

The Burton Brothers, H. Clifford and Cecil, started as employees, ended up as owners. Their mill was used by many small mine operators in the area and Burtons' Tropico became a focal point for all mining operations in the Rosamond-Mojave area. The mine prospered.

It was also in 1894, the year that Hamilton came to the desert, that W. W. Bowers prospected on the Little Buttes—later called Bowers Hill and then Standard Hill—just southwest of Mojave. The claim here was Bowers' Exposed Treasure mine; and on nearby Soledad Mountain were filed the Karma, the Queen Esther, the Elephant, the Echo, and the Gray Eagle. Active during this period were Harvey and Seely Mudd, who later became internationally famous miners. George Holmes traced the float up the side of Soledad Mountain and the Silver Queen —later the famed Golden Queen—was founded. The Golden Queen sold for three and a half million dollars.

Today all the mines are quiet, the big stamp mill at Tropico is stilled, the bleached headframes sing a sad song in the afternoon winds.

*A sketch by John W. Burgess of the Museum
and Mine at Tropico.
Tours of the Mine are offered.*

But thanks to an interest in California history, much of the savor of the old mining days has been retained. Burton's Tropico Mine is still open and operating—not as a producing mine, but as a mining museum. There is nothing quite like it in southern California.

Glen Settle, who, with his wife Dorene Burton Settle, now operates the property, was faced with a problem in 1956 when the mining operations ceased. Perhaps it was a ghost town in Nevada that decided the fate of the mine. . .

"We were making regular business trips to Hawthorne, Nevada," Settle recalls. "One trip we decided to come back over Lucky Boy Pass and visit old Aurora. On the road into the ghost town the sunlight flashed on something on a hill. We stopped and investigated, and found a couple of dozen beautiful sun-purpled whisky flasks. We started collecting old bottles that day and from that interest was born our liking for antiques and, of course, the museum idea."

So the Burton Tropico Mine became Goldcamp. The Settles acquired all the old, historic buildings they could find and moved them to the site. Here they have become stage stations, assay offices, post office—many of them performing today the same duties they did sixty years ago.

"Our mine was down to 900 feet, with working off of each 100 foot level," Settle explains. "There are miles of tunnels. We wanted to have the mine open to the public but liability insurance was prohibitive. So we opened up just the ground level of the mine, screened off the shaft so people can look down (and it's a spooky, awesome look) into the 900-foot shaft, and see some 200 feet of stoping, a big cavity where we took out ore."

Many of the tools are still in place. Here, close at hand, is some of the valuable $40 ore. Outside the mine stand the cyanide tanks and the mill. The mine is pleasant by winter (wear a sweater) and cool by summer. In summer Goldcamp is closed

*There is still water at Willow Springs
but nothing like the free flowing spring that
stood here in the old days.*

because the old buildings are not air conditioned—but the mine is, by nature, and visitors hate to leave.

There is a splendid mining museum at Goldcamp now, displaying old photographs of the area, rich ore samples, firearms, old bottles and mining mementos.

In a small art gallery on the grounds local artists display their desert paintings, sketches and water colors. There is a snack bar, parking, rest rooms. Last year 15,000 visitors paid admission to Goldcamp and the mine tour.

Willow Springs lies west and north of Burton's Tropico Mine. The Beale family owned the site when Ezra Hamilton bought it in 1900. Today it is private property and greatly changed, mainly because much of the flow of water has ceased—perhaps due to the Tehachapi earthquake. Hamilton's two-story stone hotel has been pared down to one-story following the quake, and several of the outbuildings are cracked and empty. Not far away, to the east and on a rise, is the shell of the old Willow Springs school. Indians used the springs and camped here. An Indian cemetery was unearthed when Hamilton was building his health resort, and even today arrowheads and beads can be found on the surface following a hard rain.

Just north of Willow Springs, and off on the right side of the highway that runs to Tehachapi, are the ruins of the old Cactus Queen Mine. Here is a mineral lode anomaly: the Cactus Queen produced silver; on the opposite side of the ridge was a gold-producing mine.

Along Backus Road to the east of the highway, and on the north side of the road, there is, first, an old Indian camping area with many bedrock mortars and hide-dressing stones, and a short distance beyond, an old salt cave where the desert Indians stored salt from the Koehn Dry Lake area and then traded it to the coastal Indians.

Continuing east we skirt to the north around the bulk of

*View of Willow Springs today—quiet and
sleepy—Sixty years ago it was a
booming health resort.*

Soledad Mountain. There is a fine view of the mining complex, but this is private property and not open to the public.

South from Soledad Mountain is Gem Hill, a famous and popular site with all southern California rockhounds. Here, in great quantities, were dug agate and a kind of jade. Digging in the area brought the discovery of petrified palm root, highly praised by rockhounds for its polishing qualities. South along this road brings us past the original fire clay deposits found by Dr. L. A. Crandall in the 1870's. Today the old clay pits are marked only by thousands of broken bottles and shattered tin cans where desert plinkers have practiced with rifles.

There are many prospect holes and old headframes in this area. A word of warning. There have been serious accidents in the old mines here. Recently a young man tried to jump across a yawning shaft mouth. He failed, fell and rolled hundreds of feet down a dark, rubble-choked mining shaft. He was seriously injured and his rescue took many hours.

Property owners try to keep the old tunnels and shafts on their land boarded up or screened over. But vandals pry away such barriers and explore the diggings. This is a foolhardy endeavor. Old mines are dangerous. If you have an inquisitive nature, visit the mine at Tropico. It is well-lighted, safe to walk through, and if you want a thrill, lean over and peer down into that 900-foot shaft.

If you would explore these hills, observe private property signs and stay away from abandoned diggings.

It is highly unlikely that you'll find any rich gold ore in your rambles here, but one never knows.

Goldcamp, with its antiques and old photographs and older buildings and relics, is a link with the yesterday of mining in southern California. It offers a kind of history not taught in school, and yet a history that gives a true and deeper appreciation of how the Golden State earned its name.

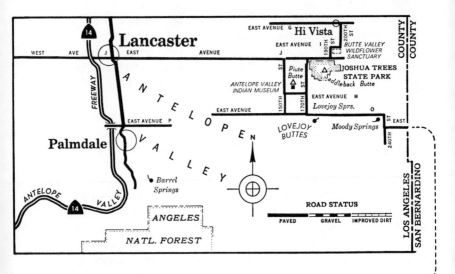

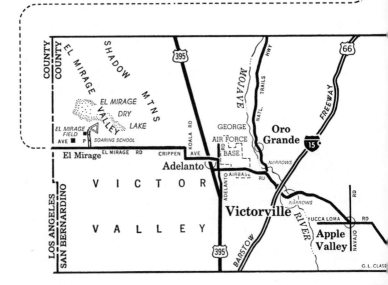

VI INDIANS LIVED ON OLD PIUTE BUTTE

Best by winter. But you'll find the sailplanes
at work much of the year. The wildflowers will be
out in spring; the desert tortoises appear then, too.

AT FIRST they looked like fallen leaves, caught up in the warm spiral of a winter whirlwind, borne aloft to twinkle in the desert sky.

Yellow and red, the leaves winked and sparkled in the wan sunlight. But then there were added leaves: green and blue and silver.

What once were leaves turned into silent airplanes, sword-bladed wings, spiraling high above the desert, hungrily seeking the warm updrafts. These were sailplanes, gliders, towed aloft from El Mirage Field, now seeking the lifting winds to carry them higher and farther, tiptoeing across the desert sky, looking for invisible steps to climb.

On almost any fair weekend in winter you'll find the sky crowded with sailplanes out over the El Mirage country. They circle in a great spiraled column, like migrating predators, noiseless, feeding greedily on the thermals.

The Antelope Valley country by January is filled with surprises. Here is a state park, here a museum, here a lake. The buttes, stained purple with haze and distance, provide a color contrast to the dun and ochres of the desert. But there is an exhilaration in the tall sky, the parade of buttes, the ragged horizon line of Joshua trees.

The Indians once were here, living in the purple-stained buttes, seeking water at Barrel and Moody and Lovejoy springs.

Experts say that if archaeologists worked for a dozen years

*The Antelope Valley Indian Museum is nestled
up close to Piute Butte east of Lancaster.*

they couldn't find all the ancient Indian material around the Lovejoy Buttes. Some of what has been found in the area is on display at a most uncommon desert site, the Antelope Valley Indian Museum.

No one should visit the Valley without pausing here, this special outpost on the shoulder of Piute Butte, to see the artifacts of primitive man.

The museum is venerable. In 1928 artist H. Arden Edwards started construction of what would eventually be this pleasant institution. It was small at first, and Edwards glamorized the finds on display with folklore and legend.

Mrs. Grace Oliver took an active interest in the museum starting in 1938. She planned many improvements, added much material that she had collected during years of interest in Indian life.

But when the new museum was completed, the war interrupted. With gasoline rationing, few people could drive the distance out to the remote site. During the war the museum was open and busy, but most of the visitors were military personnel who came in trucks and buses from military outposts.

After the war the museum began to earn its reputation as a fine exhibition of California Indian material. Few other institutions in the state display as much on the California Indians as the Antelope Valley site. Mrs. Oliver worked long hours to improve the displays, to vary them, to visit other museums all over the world.

At first there was no road to the museum. Edwards had built on the site of a lonesome homestead. He decorated the interior walls and ceilings with painting and kachina designs. The building perches over a natural rock formation.

"Piute Butte," reflects Mrs. Oliver sadly. "There never were any Piutes living in the Antelope Valley."

Mrs. Oliver obtained the extensive Irving S. Cobb collection

—Don Dwiggins photo

*From the sailplane miles of desert country
spreads out beneath. The pilot must be careful
to keep enough altitude to return to the home
base when the flight is finished, otherwise
a rugged landing could be experienced.*

of Plains Indian material, the Lackland family basket collection. A large amount of material excavated by A. R. Sanger along the Santa Barbara and Malibu coasts and on the Channel Islands is on exhibit. There is much early Southwest material here: Hohokam, Anasazi, Hopi, Navajo, Zuni, Apache.

Some of the ancient pottery on display is considered priceless by museum experts. Some of the early grass materials are almost one-of-a-kind items.

For those who picture Indian artifacts as being only arrowheads, there are hundreds of these—Plains Indians blades and the more interesting California and Southwest projectile points.

Baskets, old and new, are displayed here, with reeds and grasses on hand showing how baskets were fashioned.

The collection is so extensive and so important that a visit to the Antelope Valley Indian Museum has been woven into the regular curriculum of Lancaster and desert area schools. Thus, the visits are regular during the week in the winter months. A close-at-hand look at authentic southern California Indian material is uncommon, and here there is room enough and much to see.

In 1964, after a combination of things, Mrs. Oliver closed the museum. Her husband had died a short time before; her health was a problem; upkeep costs were spiraling; and there was talk that Los Angeles County might purchase the museum.

For three years Mrs. Oliver listened to the complaints of educators, students, parents, museum officials, neighbors, strangers. All asked that the museum be reopened, and in 1967 it was. Reaction was immediate. More than 1,500 visitors a month came to the off-the-beaten-path museum, to spend an hour with the mother-of-pearl fishhooks, the soapstone effigies, the stonework, the quillwork, bones and baubles, and baskets.

Now there is South American material on display and also Alaskan material. The scope of the museum has grown. The

*One of the more startling displays in the
Roy Rogers Museum in Apple Valley is Rogers
white convertible outfitted with six-guns for
door handles and steer horns for bumpers.*

cases are modern, well-lighted. The museum is air conditioned. There is a road and a good one.

To get to the museum, and to start this winter byway, drive east from Lancaster along Avenue J. It is quite a distance out to 150th Street, maybe fifteen miles. Here you turn south on 150th Street for three miles, to Avenue M. Then east again, and follow the signs to the museum. The museum is built on the side of Piute Butte (it was once Peck's Butte, named after an early-day settler). The row of hills on the south is called Lovejoy Buttes. The area is dotted with Indian sites. There is a subdivision here now — Lake Los Angeles.

The museum is open daily from 10:00 A.M. to 5:00 P.M. There is a small admission charge. Adjacent are picnic grounds. Curators are Lewis and Lillian Brown.

At the drinking fountain in the parking area, small birds line up to drink. Almost daily, when there are no cars around, a lone roadrunner comes to the faucet to take water.

Then drive east from the museum on Avenue M to 170th Street turn north for a three-mile drive up to Saddleback Butte and a visit to Joshua Trees State Park.

A new park, it was dedicated in 1960 with the idea of preserving some of the virgin Joshua tree forest that exists in the butte country. It lacks proper funding and therefore does not yet have a proposed self-guided nature trail, an interpretive center and a naturalist program. But these things will come. The camping and picnic facilities are temporary, but they are adequate for the smog-weary who like to come here for the night full of stars and the gentle floodtide of winter winds.

Those who come, too, have a chance to glimpse the typical desert wildlife that lives here. Kit foxes are tame enough to approach the evening campfire circle. Kangaroo rats are common, as are desert chipmunks. By spring the desert tortoise will be out, but in January he's burrowed away during his strange hibernation period. Roadrunners parade boldly through the park. Sometimes hikers through the 2,720-acre preserve see sidewinders or the green Mojave rattlesnake. These are to be carefully avoided; they are both venomous.

Bird watchers enjoy the park's collection of native wild birds. Here they'll spyglass the hunting hawks, they'll chart the antics of the cactus thrasher.

Not too well known, not overly used, the Joshua Trees State Park has an excellent future. It is a pleasure place for Southlanders to come for a picnic lunch. There is a great pastel panorama of desert that spreads out from the park. A walk under the Joshua trees reveals all manner of desert secrets. In springtime this region is afire with wildflowers. Nearby Hi Vista— there is a good road to Hi Vista and a store and gas station there —celebrates the blossoming miracle with a wildflower festival.

Just north of Joshua Trees State Park is the Butte Valley Wildflower Sanctuary. It is a county wildflower preserve.

South now, along 170th Street to Avenue O and the carnival setting of a real estate development.

Run east on Avenue O toward the sunrise. The road is a good one, it jogs at Moody Springs, 240th Street (another Indian site), and heads east again on Avenue P (El Mirage Road).

A short distance inside the San Bernardino County line is El Mirage Field. The great smooth complex of El Mirage Dry Lake lies to the north, and if you hanker for unpaved desert roads, you can try driving out to it. You might see here any manner of strange aircraft taking off and landing. Some days you'll see small, homemade airplanes testing their wings . . . or gyrocopters . . . or gliders.

But most of the activity at El Mirage Field concerns sailplaning. For a fee, a sturdy aircraft will tow you glider aloft. At the proper altitude you have the option of release. You are master of the sky then, you and a slender pair of wings and the whistle of air slipping past.

On weekends you'll find gliders lined up waiting for their powered escort into the sky. You'll find cars parked near the field with spectators watching, silenced by the spectacle and beauty of the sailplanes at work.

And here, for a fee, you can be taken up for a short sight-seeing flight over the eastern Antelope Valley, El Mirage Valley and Victor Valley.

On east now, through Adelanto and the impressive military outpost of George Air Force Base—a fighter field.

On to Victorville, through Victorville (stay off the freeway and watch for signs to Apple Valley).

This is still desert country. More used and less attractive than the country around Joshua Trees State Park, the area still has a certain charm.

You'll drive through Apple Valley a way before you come to the Apple Valley Inn and Roy Rogers' personal museum.

A word here: if you are a Roy Rogers fan, or a motion picture buff, or if you like to peer in the window at how celebrities live, you'll enjoy this modern neat, orderly museum. You'll not mind an admission price to look at Roy Rogers' and Dale Evans' lives, in photographs, in mementos. You'll be impressed that they took the trouble to stuff and display Trigger, Rogers' faithful horse of 188 films; you'll boggle at Rogers' gleaming white, Western convertible, decked out with six-guns for door handles, horse heads for light switches, steerhorns for bumpers, uphol-stered in hand-tooled leather studded with silver dollars.

If you are a Roy Rogers fan, you'll enjoy the homey touch of a reproduction of the Rogers' dining room, the table set for dinner. You'll thrill to Rogers' big-game trophies.

If you are not a Rogers fan, you might think that Trigger deserved a better fate, that the gleaming white convertible is low camp in questionable taste, and that polar bears may make a fine trophy but are becoming almost extinct in the wilds.

Still, Roy Rogers and Dale Evans are highly attractive people, enjoy incredible popularity, and have here presented their lives in as pleasing a format as could be devised.

Take the time, while you are in this area, to visit the Apple Valley Inn, a showplace of the desert and offering an excellent dining room.

By now, if you have spent just the right amount of time at the Antelope Valley Desert Museum, Joshua Trees State Park, El Mirage Field and the Roy Rogers Museum, you'll find that the winter's day has somehow run out. Your best course back to the Los Angeles area is via the Cajon Pass route—U.S. Highway 66 and 395, Interstate 15.

But if you can, linger in the area, spend another day out here. You have before you and close at hand the mysteries of Lucerne Valley, the charm of Calico, back roads to Big Bear and on to the High Desert.

By January the desert will implore you to stay awhile, to lose yourself in the purple mists of distance, to follow this road to the horizon and that one on beyond.

And mark well where you've been on the map. Chances are you'll want to return, if only to watch the roadrunner drink from the faucet, or to see the silvery sailplanes in the sky, or to gaze, bemused but overwhelmed, at that utterly fantastic convertible.

84

VII DESERT MUSEUM HOLDS SECRET OF THE PAST

The museum in Bloomington is open almost daily. The sites it urges you to visit are deep desert sites, best seen by cooler weather. Some of them are on rough roads.

DR. GERALD A. SMITH of Bloomington, Calif., knows where there is a herd of mammoths.

The mammoth was a prehistoric elephant, one variety of which reached the enormous height of fourteen feet and had great sweeping tusks. It has not been seen in San Bernardino County for at least 50,000 years, maybe longer. But it once was here. . .

Dr. Smith's herd, of course, consists only of fossil remains, but even so, such knowledge is unusual and could be enormously important. Particularly so if archaeologists could find, imbedded amongst the fossil bones of the prehistoric elephants, evidences of early man—such as charcoal from an ancient hearth or stone weapons. This would strengthen the already-held notion that man in the West did live concurrently with some of the big, vanished animals of prehistoric times, like the giant sloth and the mammoth.

The fact that Dr. Smith has this knowledge surprises none of his friends. Smith has been uncovering unusual facts about San Bernardino County for many years. As director of the dynamic San Bernardino County Museum, he concerns himself with such things as the location of the desert campsites occupied over thousands of years by the aboriginal people who lived here. He is knowledgeable about the many secret places where these people did their rock writings—pictographs and petroglyphs. He knows where the crude fist axes of early man can be found. He has

85

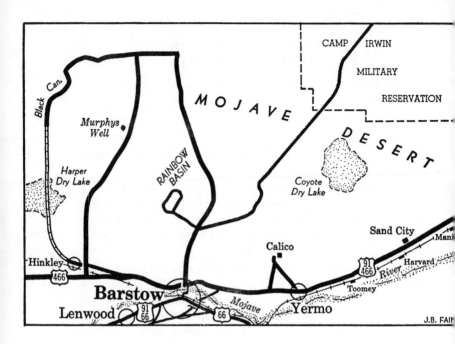

charted the shoreline of prehistoric lakes, like old Lake Manix, that dried and dwindled until today it is desert country, dotted here and there by recognizable dry lakes. He knows where there are fossils, some imbedded in the tough matrix of clay or stone, others weathering but naked in the wash of desert wind.

The San Bernardino County Museum is the focus for this knowledge. Here, in attractive, interesting displays, are the material that Smith and his fellow museum workers have collected, sorted, identified, dated and written about. Materials that include items of the lithic (stone) industries of the long procession of people who have lived in the great San Bernardino County outback; samples of pictographs and petroglyphs; fossils; rocks and minerals; animals and birds and reptiles. The San Bernardino County Museum is a distillation of what there is in the county; it is a repository, a condensation, a source of knowledge.

"If you are planning on a trip into the San Bernardino Mountains," Smith might say, "we suggest that you come here first and, for example, see the bird displays. They are all identified. Then when you see a particular bird in the mountains you know whether it is a junco or a flicker or a hawk. Your outing has taken on more meaning. And your visit will be more pleasant because of your knowledge."

Smith is anxious for southern Californians to use San Bernardino County—to see it, savor it, scratch around in it. The biggest county in the continental United States, it holds all manner of surprises. The museum at Bloomington is the key to many of these surprises.

Using this key it is possible to unlock many strange gates into the county's back country where such mysteries can be explored by byway explorers in passenger cars.

Pictographs and petroglyphs? There are desert sites off the

*A row of what appear to be big horn sheep are
pecked into the rocks in Black Canyon
north of Barstow. Large area here is dotted
with Indian rock writing.*

highway but still on good paved roads where the explorer can look and marvel and photograph.

An Indian desert campground? No problem. A sizeable one lies almost on a paved road, easy to visit.

A fossil bed? A fine unpaved loop road penetrates one of the most interesting desert fossil areas in southern California.

Even an early man site can be approached by passenger cars, close enough for a look, if not an actual communion with the relics of 5,000 to 50,000 years ago.

All these unusual byway advantages are possible through a study of the San Bernardino County museum, a most uncommon place . . .

For seventy-five years the San Bernardino County Pioneer Society had had the dream of a county museum. In later years the desire was also felt and expressed by the San Bernardino Historical Society. The problems were not unusual: needed were money, a site, a staff.

Then in May of 1952 the San Bernardino Museum Association was formed, monies were collected, and the goal became a little more definite. The old San Bernardino mission *asistencia* was acquired and given to the county; the Sepulveda adobe in Yucaipa was similarly saved from destruction.

Then the Bloomington Dads' Club, in a project to build more classroom space for the Bloomington School District, then on double session, conceived a workable program whereby emergency school buildings could be passed on to the Museum as they were withdrawn from school use. On Sunday, July 14, 1957, the new San Bernardino County Museum was dedicated and opened to the public. The museum is now assisted by county funds, but still depends to a great degree on volunteer help.

As the museum grew, important gifts were received. One of the most important of these was the Wilson C. Hanna collection of more than 200,000 bird eggs. Probably the largest collection

*Early man country—this is the look of the land
around the high water mark of vanished
Lake Manix, a prehistoric body of water that once
knew prehistoric man around its perimeter.
National Geographic is investigating this site.*

of its kind in the world, it is flanked in the museum by cases carrying preserved specimens of the birds that live in or migrate through San Bernardino County. These have been prepared and identified by ornithologist-taxidermist Eugene Cardiff.

A collection of snakes was accumulated. Mexican art was donated. Historical items from San Bernardino County were collected and displayed. There is a grouping of mounted mammals of the county including two rams, a ewe and a lamb of the rare bighorn sheep family.

Still there is strong emphasis on archaeology here; partly because of the influence of Smith, party because of the fact that San Bernardino County is so rich in the lore.

There are memorable sites in the county from the historian's and the archaeologist's point of view. For example, it was from Newberry Cave that *atlatl* (the throwing stick that preceded the bow and arrow) material and sloth remains were found. From the shores of prehistoric Lake Manix Miss Ruth Simpson, archaeologist of the Southwest Museum and the San Bernardino County Museum, has found the stone implements of early man. There is a fantastic "wall of rock writing" in the Black Canyon area north of Barstow. Fossils abound in Rainbow Basin.

Formerly attached to the Southwest Museum of Los Angeles and now affiliated with the San Bernardino County Museum is the Archaeological Survey Association. In February 1963 the Museum dedicated the Archaeological Survey Association of Southern California's Research Center for the Study of Early Man. It is here that the collecting, sorting, classifying, photographing of early man material from all over southern California will take place. The A.S.A. Research Center is designed to function in cooperation with all other interested museums in the region. Material thus will be on loan to the A.S.A. while the necessary research work is being done; then it can be returned to the parent museum for permanent display.

—Photo by Vernon James

*In addition to looking for fossils in
weather-sculptured Rainbow Basin north of
Barstow, there are some fine hills for sliding down:
a dusty sport.*

The A.S.A. is what its name implies: a survey group. Members from all corners of southern California are schooled in making preliminary studies of various areas, to look for the tell-tale signs of early man habitation. (The group considers any habitation evidence older than 5000 years to be that of early man.)

And since San Bernardino County's ranging desert wilderness is rich in such early man deposits, the new home for the A.S.A. seems a natural one.

Major project now for the group is the summation of the survey of the Lake Manix complex. There was a time when almost all of the San Bernardino desert country was lakes and marshland, heavy with grass and graze, populated by large herds of herbivorous animals as well as their predators. The possibility of finding both fossil remains and the evidence of herd-hunting tribes of aboriginal people are excellent.

It is toward such research that the A.S.A. is dedicated. Those interested in becoming members of such a group need only write to the organization in care of the museum at Bloomington to secure the necessary information.

Using the Museum as a key, let us visit that site first, then, understanding more of what we will see later, follow the byway trail that stretches out into the back country.

The San Bernardino County Museum is most easily reached by driving east from the Los Angeles area over the San Bernardino Freeway to the Cedar Avenue turnoff in Bloomington. Drive two blocks south on Cedar Avenue to Orange Street. Here turn east again and follow this street to its end some three blocks away. You'll immediately recognize the museum by some of the larger objects on display: a jet airplane, a military tank, a locomotive and a caboose. Here, in a complex of rambling buildings, is the museum.

The museum has been open every day since its dedication in

1957 except for Thanksgiving and Christmas: a fantastic public service record. In 1968-69 the museum had more than 200,000 visits—a large number by school children who came from all over San Bernardino, Riverside and Los Angeles Counties.

Particularly interesting are the artifacts taken from various archaeological sites in cases flanking the main assembly hall. Maps with the displays help orient the traveler to the sites in the field.

Tying in with material on display at the museum, director Smith has suggested the following collection of scenic and interesting sites for byway explorers.

The Indians of the San Bernardino mountain country were mainly the Serrano, a name that means mountains. A typical "late" Indian campsite in the San Bernardino Mountains is at Rock Camp. This is located north of Lake Arrowhead on the paved portion of the old Toll Road which runs around the east side of Lake Mojave and then north. There is a ranger station at Rock Camp and beside it a good dirt road runs east for a short distance to a cairn and a historical marker.

This plaque calls attention to the *metate* holes in the rocks nearby. The plaque's terminology is incorrect. The holes are more correctly known as bedrock mortars, but regardless, this is an old, permanent Indian campsite of long duration. There is much darkened earth here, indicating years of cooking fires, and many permanent mortar holes in the rocks where the Indian women ground their acorns into meal.

Here was, in Indian times, a perfect Indian campsite. Sheltered, supplied with water, acorns and game, the camp was probably occupied until the coming of the white man.

For a fossil site, one that has yielded, for example, camel bones 11 million years old, as well as other bones and fossil shells, there is no better place than Rainbow Basin.

To reach this site turn north out of Barstow on the Fort

Irwin Road, drive this paved route 5.1 miles to a good dirt road leading to the west. Along this three miles is the northward trending Fossil Loop Road running back into the Rainbow Basin. The chalky bluffs here are multicolored and weathered into attractive shapes. The road is narrow in many places and offers few turnouts for parking. But from such you can scramble over the hills looking for bits of bone and shell that have weathered out of the formation.

For a site where petroglyphs can be found in profusion, there is Black Canyon reached by two routes that are suitable for passenger cars. One runs north out of Hinkley, up past Murphy's Well, then east to the Petroglyph site. The other is up the Fort Irwin Road out of Barstow, past the turnoff west into the fossil site for about a mile, then left on a dirt road that runs generally north for sixteen miles, then turn left, crossing the Hinkley approach road, and on west into the petroglyph area.

The Black Canyon petroglyphs are chipped into a low rock wall at the edge of the hills. There is a cove here, set back from the access road, and a dirt road departs from the main byway and reaches back into the cove. It is not a dangerous side road, but drive off the pavement only where other cars have been. It is almost impossible to get into trouble here, but it is back country. You are, at the Black Canyon site, some thirty miles from civilization. This might be terrifying for some—but it needn't be. Black Canyon attracts a certain number of visitors almost every day of the year; on a fair spring week-end, you will not be alone.

Dr. Smith's suggestion of an early man site requires little more imagination and a little more caution for drivers of passenger cars.

East of Barstow there is a town called Yermo. The agriculture check station for people entering the state is here. East of Yermo, and north of the railroad station of Toomey, you can see a high tension line running off to the northeast. In the foreground this line climbs up over a low ridge of hills. Atop this low ridge, according to expert Smith, there is considerable evidence of the rough stone flaking and crude tools that typify early man's lithic industry. This highland, the Museum and the A.S.A. are convinced, was once the campsite of prehistoric people. It sat on the edge of old Lake Manix when that body of water was at its highest level.

It may be difficult to drive to the edge of this site, although a side road exists, because of the present freeway construction in the area. But Dr. Smith reminds, much of this area east of the Calico Hill and up toward Coyote Dry Lake is "early man country."

See the museum—see the country. This might be the guideline to this byway outing. Explorers with more desert travel knowledge and with jeeps or similar transportation, will probably be inclined to go farther afield in the San Bernardino County back country as a result of their museum visit.

It is an enormous run of country. Dr. Smith will tell you that you cannot see it all in detail in a lifetime. But he's working at it.

VIII POKING INTO THE DALE MINING DISTRICT

Best visited by winter or early spring. Trip described can be completed in a day but with jeep or truck there are many beckoning side roads. Take normal precautions.

THE CALIFORNIA DESERT is speckled with the sites of camps that never quite made it. Most were mining outposts where, at first, there was boom. A year later, after the rude wooden buildings had gone up, the boom turned to bust and the people pulled out, leaving everything behind them.

Some were more substantial outposts, towns that lived more than a year and that gave up millions in gold and silver. Witness Cerro Gordo and Panamint City.

The mining fraternity, the earth grubbers and their families, the hangers-on, the storekeepers and the others, were all boomers. They moved from camp to camp and they moved often. Always they were chasing the rainbow, the big bonanza that would be permanent. They moved and each time they stopped they gave their towns fancy names like Esmeralda and Aurora.

Dale was different.

When the people moved away, Dale went right along with them. It was a town that couldn't be shaken loose.

It was in terrible country—water was almost non-existent, there were no shade trees and civilization was days away.

The Dales boomed and flourished but in time, as with all the desert outposts, the string of Dales ended too. The scars are there, if you look for them, where once stood Old Dale, Dale the Second and Dale the Third. People lived in the inhospitable country—where almost no one lives even today—and conducted the usual commerce. Babies were born and somehow survived.

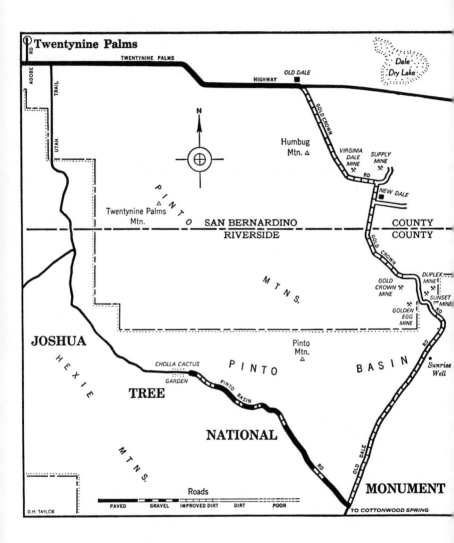

These were primitive camps, the Dales, and the country they dominated is still remote and rugged. But there is a good dirt road that pierces the region and on a balmy winter day it is a fair land to visit. The wind can be chill late of an afternoon and when there are storm clouds, it is best to avoid the muddy tracks.

The Dale mining district is in San Bernardino County, east of Twentynine Palms and the Joshua Tree National Monument.

To get there simply follow the Twentynine Palms Highway through that community and on east fourteen miles to the intersection with the Gold Crown Road which leads south. This will be your main avenue of exploration and its condition during the first mile or two will give you a good idea of what the majority of your off-pavement excursion will be like. Don't attempt the drive without a spare tire. In fact take all the normal off pavement driving precautions. If you are spooked about driving on dirt roads, make sure there are two cars in a caravan. It's a long walk to the nearest service station.

According to the most persistent but tentative history, the site of Old Dale is at the junction of the Twentynine Palms Highway and the Gold Crown Road.

The Valley Mountain topographical map sheet—issued in 1956—shows structures on both the north and south side of the Twentynine Palms Highway at that junction. No structures stand here that date back to the 1883 operation, although there is rubble and some concrete foundations.

Ronald Dean Miller, in his interesting paperback, *Mines of the High Desert,* published by La Siesta Press, reports that the camp of Virginia Dale—possibly named after the first child to be born in the camp—was located where it was because there was water: "There, a well was dug and an arrastre built to mill the ores of the district. Here the town grew up."

The sites of all three Dales have been combed and dug by

The cyanide tanks at the Virgina Dale Mine are still intact but vandals have lugged off all the transportable machinery.

bottle hunters. We did find a number of very old tins cans, soldered ones, hinting an age before 1900.

Follow the Gold Crown Road south approximately 4.5 miles and you'll arrive at the site of the Virginia Dale Mine, founded in 1885 by Johnny Wilson and Tom Lyons. This was Dale the Second.

Only at Dale the Second are there any town buildings standing, and these are being steadily picked to pieces by the desert winds and vandals.

In 1916 the State Mineralogist report described the mine thus: ". . . the mine is equipped with a Lane mill, built about six or seven years ago. This mill was not operated to any great extent, only about 1000 to 1500 tons of ore having been treated. Active work was commenced on this group in the summer of 1890 at which time a five-stamp mill was moved there from Twentynine Palms."

The Virginia Dale Mine consists of six claims in the Black Mountains, an arm of the Pinto Mountains.

And what about that necessity—water?

It was piped all the way from the well at Old Dale—nearly five miles.

Lulu Rasmussen O'Neal, area historian, has written: "Although one of the Dales is said to have had a population at one time of 3,000, the population of Dale township in 1900 was 63, fluctuating thereafter to 41 in 1910 and only eight in 1920."

To explore the Virginia Dale Mine, park on the Gold Crown Road and walk back to the mine—no great distance. The road to the mine is very sandy and unless you have a jeep and are a skilled back country driver, you could get into trouble here. An additional word of advice: there are open mine shafts in the area. If you have pets or small children, keep them in hand.

Vandals have wrought as much damage to the old mill and

The weather headframe still stands at the
Virginia Dale Mine — the mine that
supported Dale the Second.

mine as anything—vandals and metal thieves, but a good deal is left.

On the hill to the northwest of the mill are some of the living areas of the mining camp. The old tin cans will tell you that this was quite a settlement for a short while. There are still traces of fine hardwood flooring in the old mine office building. A large bunkhouse when we visited the site was about to collapse. Vandals had chopped away supporting beams for firewood.

The Gold Crown Road now curves toward the east. Just as it makes the bend to the south again is the access road up to the Supply Mine, sitting on a bench in the Pintos.

It is possible to drive to the beginning of the access road; then rocks and ruts are the barricade—not sand. Don't tear your car to pieces trying to get back to the mine. Walk up the hill to the site.

None of the histories report exactly when the Supply Mine was founded, nor who found the rich claim.

The Supply Mine was the cause of Dale moving for the second time. The new campsite, New Dale, or Dale the Third, is about a half mile from the mine and off on a spur from the Gold Crown Road. You'll know the site when you reach it by the acres of tin cans. The Dale Post office moved here in 1915.

At the Supply Mine several buildings still stand; in later years, at least, the mine had electricity. There is the wreckage of a large refrigerator building.

The headframe stands askew and tailings and mud are piled high. It was quite an operation in its day.

The mine, according to the State Mineralogist, "covers 350 acres and for many years was a regular producer, having yielded over $250,000 . . . ceased operations in the winter of 1915."

According to Miller the mine operated until 1917; under the ownership of United Greenwater produced $1 million in gold. The mine has been inactive since World War II and in

*This could be the site of Old Dale. Only some
rubble and foundations mark the site
of the 1883 boom camp.*

another ten years will probably be reduced to nothing but foundations and rubble.

The site of New Dale—Dale the Third—was possibly the camp with the population of 3,000 mentioned by Mrs. O'Neal. But it was also much smaller than that.

In 1919 J. Smeaton Chase wrote in *California Desert Trails:* "This Dale, I learned, was Dale the Third. As the old 'leads' or veins of ore 'peter out' and new ones are discovered, the mining camp 'follows the lead' in a literal sense. The present camp is about a dozen years old, and is supported by one good-sized gold mine, the Supply, though there are a few smaller mines in the locality. Fifty or sixty men, half a dozen women, and one badly spoiled baby made up the population at the time of my stay. The mine is a highly organized affair, with electric-lighted buildings and a water supply pumped from wells six miles away. Day and night the whirr and crash of engines goes on unceasing. It was strange to wake at night and hear the roar of machinery in that remote place. . . ."

There are a few crumbing corners of masonry left at the site of New Dale and at the Supply Mine a side hill is completely covered by old soldered cans. All have been patiently raked by collectors in the search for old bottles.

Back in the hills—fair game only for drivers of jeeps or similar vehicles—are some other mines, notably the lofty Ivanhoe, atop a peak in the Pintos. But the roads up to these sites are pure horror. Only for skillful jeep drivers.

South of the three Dales the Gold Crown Road seeks the Pinto Basin.

But first there is a low ridge of hills to be climbed. There may be a few patches of rough road here—nothing terrible but places where it would be prudent to creep along for a few feet.

A scattering of small mines in this ridge area includes the Gold Crown, Golden Egg, Sunset and Duplex, among others.

*A few ruined buildings remain at the
living quarters of Dale the Second in the
Pinto Mountains foothills.*

*Two of the dwellings at the old Supply Mine.
Vandals may have taken these down by now.
People who worked here lived below on a
flatland site at New Dale,
also known as Dale the Third.*

Finally the great sprawl of the Pinto Basin opens up, with the horizon broken to the southeast by the Eagle Mountains and to the southwest by the Hexie Range.

The road drops steeply—and again there may be a couple of rough spots—to the floor of the Basin.

At one time this valley in the Joshua Tree National Monument held a great lake and around the lake lived prehistoric man. His artifacts have been discovered and a fascinating scientific paper on the Pinto Basin has been written by Elizabeth E. Crozer Campbell and William H. Campbell, and published by the Southwest Museum. The booklet, first issued in 1935, has been reprinted.

The road passes a couple of wells—Mission Well and Sunrise Well. At the former site are the ruins of the old Mission mill.

Our dirt byway makes a junction with another dirt road leading east to several mines and the paved road running through Joshua Tree National Monument.

It is rewarding to drive this paved road north to the Cholla Cactus Garden and take the self-guiding nature trail here. Again a warning. The cholla cactus sheds its spines in clusters. These spines will easily pierce tough clothing, even canvas and thin leather shoes. Pets should be kept in the car. Small children should not be allowed to wander off by themselves. And adults should walk gingerly through the clumps of cholla. The old-timers did not nickname the stuff "jumping cactus" for nothing. The spines are so sharp they gouge you before you touch them.

The road south from the Gold Crown Road takes you to the new Joshua Tree National Monument visitors' center at Cottonwood Spring. There is a new large campground here on a flatland. The old campground in the hollow under the cottonwoods has been closed and the trees removed. They were old and rotted and park officials feared they might fall. This southern park entrance leads off Interstate 10 some twenty-five miles east of Indio.

By winter and early spring the desert is a friendly place—especially if you take along a lunch for a picnic in the sun.

Perhaps, after looking the country over, you'll decide—as most do—that you'd never want to live at any of the three Dales. But a good many people invested years here in this wilderness, made a living and raised families. They were hoping for that big bonanza. Few ever found it, but their search helped to write southern California's history.

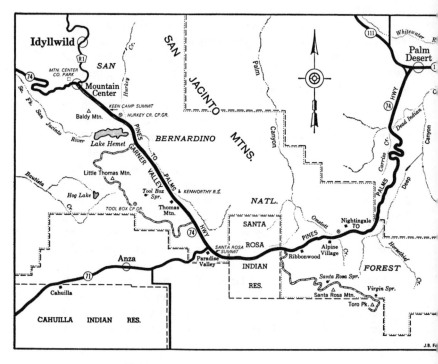

IX OFF THE SAN JACINTOS OUT INTO THE DESERT

*This one is best by spring or fall. Too much snow
can spoil the mountain part of the trip; too much
heat can diminish the desert pleasures. Many contrasts.*

THERE WAS A DAY, not so long ago, when you could stand on
one of the desert-facing spires of the San Jacinto Mountains in
Riverside County and see the flash of the afternoon sun against
the snow-topped San Francisco Peaks near Flagstaff in Arizona.

This day has gone, not that the distance has grown with the
passage of years, but because of man-made hazes.

Even so, the view from the tall San Jacintos, notably Thomas
Mountain, Santa Rosa Mountain and Toro Peak. is virtually
without compare in all of southern California. From these peaks,
where the pines and cedars crowd against a bluer sky, it is possible to reach out and examine landmarks in more than a half
dozen Southland counties, to name a score or more of lesser
mountain ranges. By night the bright jewels of dozens of communities flash skyward.

The San Jacinto Mountains are attractive by any measure. On
the wooded slopes, among the piles of boulders and sentinel
crags, climb patriarchal pines admiringly called by knowledgeable foresters "eight log trees." The cedars have been famed
since the 1860's when intruders climbed the mountains on foot
and took away pack strings of shakes and shingles. There are
wild lands here today: a state park and a wild area within the
National Forest, and both have thousands of supporters for their
wildnerness features.

It is along a single paved road through this country—and a
number of unpaved side roads—that this byway runs. The by-

109

*The pleasant, peaceful dirt road that climbs
from the Pines to Palms Highway up along the
Santa Rosa Mountains and then reaches for the
summit of Toro Peak. Many desert views are offered.*

way starts at Mountain Center in the San Jacinto Mountains, the titular beginning of the Pines-to-Palms Highway. From Mountain Center the Pines-to-Palms Highway runs south and east for thirty-six miles to a union with the Coachella Valley arm of the Colorado Desert near the community of Palm Desert.

It is an uncommon road in its passage through the labeled life zones from mile-high mountains to sea-level desert. It is an uncommon road in its history. It is uncommon in the scenery from its pavement, and in the grander scenery that lies hidden from the byway, but easily accessible from side roads on either side.

From the junction community of Mountain Center the byway climbs gently as it heads east past the entrance to old Keen Camp, where a grand resort once stood (it burned in 1943) and where an old ranger outpost dozes. Keen Camp is now an organizational camp.

South of the road is Baldy Mountain and hidden in its upper reaches are a number of attractive mountain meadows, ideal for recreation. Unfortunately the access road crosses private land— public use must wait until a public road can be built.

Keen Camp Summit is passed—4,917 feet—and the highway, State Highway 74, starts down the hill.

On either side is the historic sprawl of the Garner Cattle Co. Once the lands of the original white settler, Charles Thomas, who bought the lands from the Indians, the tract was acquired by the Garner Company in 1904.

Off to the left is the inviting Hurkey Creek Campground, operated by the county of Riverside. The place name pays homage to an old-time employee of the Thomas Ranch by the name of Hurkey or Herkey who was mauled by a grizzly bear and died of his wounds. The last grizzly bear was killed in these mountains in 1890.

Now a pleasant flat meadowland opens—largest in the San

*Jeffrey and Coulter pines ring the attractive
Garner Valley country and beyond, along the
northern horizon, stands the formidable Desert
Divide. Beyond is the Palm Springs country.*

Jacinto Mountains—surrounded by stands of Jeffrey and Coulter pines. Once this was called Thomas Valley, later that name was changed to Hemet Valley, and now it is known as Garner Valley.

More than seventy years ago ranchers from the San Jacinto Valley, on the west side of the San Jacinto Mountains, hiked up the South Fork of the San Jacinto River into this pine-rimmed basin seeking a source of irrigation water. A water company was formed and in 1890 work was started on a dam. Fashioned of hand-hewn blocks of native stone hoisted into place by a primitive steam engine, the barrier trapped the upper runoff into the South Fork and formed Lake Hemet.

On Forest Service land overlooking the lake the Riverside County park department has installed three ramada-shaded picnic areas. There is year-around fishing in the lake which is stocked regularly. On water company land there are fee facilities for camping, trailers, etc.

Less than a mile beyond the lake, on the south side of the highway, a side road labeled the Little Thomas Mountain Road, reaches toward the higher mountain country.

This byway, unpaved and rough but passable for passenger cars, climbs to the rocky spine of the Thomas Mountain country. The area east of the Little Thomas Mountain Road is within the Forest Service's annual fire closure. The road climbs to a junction, turns here to the east, passes Little Thomas Mountain and enters a picturesque, unspoiled pine forest. There is a small, semi-improved Forest Service campground here named Thomas Mountain. Just beyond, a spur road runs up to the summit of the peak. Here, scratching at the sky, is a spidery sixty-foot-tall metal lookout tower used by the Forest Service only in cases of emergency. It has the reputation of being a terrifying place during a hot lightning storm.

Thomas Mountain is one of the viewpoints that enhance this country. All the mountains in Riverside, Orange and San Diego

Small Hemet Lake, backed up behind the stone dam built in the 1890s, offers year-around fishing.

Counties are spread below this vantage point. The dome of the great observatory at Palomar burns in the sunlight; the Lagunas in far San Diego County seem close at hand. The Anza, Cahuilla and Terwilliger Valley country just below is sharp in detail. Tiny Hog Lake on the Ramona Indian Reservation is a landmark. Cahuilla Mountain, to the west, is purpled in the rising haze.

Past the summit of Thomas Mountain this forest road continues through attractive pine woods to the east, passes the little Tool Box Campground, and then starts its descent through mature chaparral to the highway again.

Back up the Pines-to-Palms Highway, along the length of it we have just bypassed, is the turnoff to the north to the Kenworthy ranger station of the San Jacinto district of the San Bernardino National Forest. The station takes its name from the vanished boom camp of Kenworthy which came up between 1896 and 1904 in Pine Meadows just to the east. Kenworthy was made up of salted mines and stock speculation, according to mining experts, but still it attracted a population large enough to support a school, a two-story hotel, and of course saloons. Often prospected, the San Jacinto Mountains have yet to yield any rewarding show of gold. And nothing remains of old Kenworthy.

From this north rim of Garner Valley—you'll claim it would make a good motion picture setting and indeed many westerns were shot here and around Keen Camp in the 1930's—it is possible to look high along the northern horizon at the sawedge of rocky peaks known locally as the Desert Divide. There are no roads there and few trails. It is best suited to its shyest inhabitants: the desert bighorn sheep.

Past the little mountain community of Thomas Mountain we run on southeast now and come to the junction with State Highway 71. This good high-gear road leads southwest through the little settlements of Anza and Cahuilla, through their valleys and the lands of the Cahuilla Indian Reservation, on down to

*Desert Steve Ragsdale's log cabin atop
Santa Rosa Mountain has a man-sized fireplace,
is snug against the wild winter weather that often
visits here. It is less than an hour's drive to the
deep desert in the Coachella Valley area.*

Aguanga. There was once a trial from the Indian rancheria at Anza into the Garner Valley region. Thomas made it into a wagon road and it became the first access route into the San Jacinto Mountains.

Leaving Garner Valley the Pines-to-Palms Highways descends gently to the east and makes the first definite statement in its passage through the life zones here. The road crosses the Canadian, the Transition, the Upper Sonoran and the Lower Sonoran. The pines become less numerous and great green oaks begin to shade the hills and gather around the cienegas.

A side road leads to the Santa Rosa Indian Reservation where there is a picturesque old chapel and graveyard, but do not enter Indian Reservation lands without *written* permission.

Just beyond, where the red shank or ribbonwood begins to make its most determined showing, there is a turnoff onto Santa Rosa Mountain.

This sometimes rough, sometimes dusty side road climbs through the ribbonwood, passes an old miner's outpost, begins to work its way up the west face of Santa Rosa Mountain. The switchbacks are not difficult, and in a few miles the comforting edge of the pine forest is gained. A short distance beyond is the best drinking water in all the San Jacintos.

You'll find this natural treat at Santa Rosa Springs where the Forest Service has built a three-unit campground. Fill your canteen here, the sweet water will taste good all day.

Just beyond, the dirt road enters private land—the road is still open to the public—once owned by Desert Steve Ragsdale, king of the entire section across the summit of Santa Rosa Mountain. At one time Ragsdale, with bright colored paints, wrote on the rocks and trees here. But no one was offended. For Ragsdale created brief, pungent poems about the dangers of forest fire.

The road continues east, crosses a section of Forest Service land, and then enters the Santa Rosa Indian Reservation. You'll

117

be able to drive for a short distance before the road's gated. Each time you come to a fork take the upper road. If you've a mind for a huffing and puffing hike, follow the road past the gate to the top of Toro Peak. There's a Santa Rosa legend that the top of Toro Peak is haunted, but this did not keep out the Marine Corps who built a radio relay station and a helicopter landing pad on the summit. Toro Peak, 8,716 feet, again offers some fantastic views.

Take your time as you drive back down the mountain. There will be some wildflowers out, although the wildflower season at this elevation comes late. Savor the scent of pine; collect, if you will, some of the bumper crop of pine cones that dropped last year—no one will mind. There is a small hike off this dirt road to Stump Spring and Cedar Spring; as you make your passage through the new ferns watch for quail and deer, both seek sanctuary here.

The Pines-to-Palms Highway works on down, shakes off almost all its mountain flora, embraces instead the yucca, the agave, the cactus. You'll pass real estate subdivisions and parcels of private land that have been improved. There is a small settlement and a Forest Service campground at Pinyon Flat

The road curves to the north now, heads away from Forest Service land into the desert-facing country. Cholla cactus stands on watch on the hills.

Then an engineering feat: Seven Level Hill. In this brief span the highway makes a series of spectacular switchbacks, dropping ever lower. From each arm of switchback there is an expanding panorama of the desert to the north. As the last of the hills are left behind, the road levels and drops toward an intersection with State Highway 111. This is desert palm country. The highway has kept its promise.

With the touch of winter and early spring rains still sweet on the land is the best time to visit this country of many contrasts.

X THE NEWEST ROAD INTO BORREGO SPRINGS AREA

Another cool weather trip. You'll find the rangers in
Anza-Borrego Desert State Park helpful and informative.
And remember, it's almost impossible to get lost in the park.

THERE IS A spectacular comparatively new road into the Borrego Valley of San Diego County. From the west it edges over a shoulder of the flinty wall of the San Ysidro Mountains and snakes gingerly into the valley below.

It was a long time coming: nine years. It opened in 1965. Because it offers some breathtaking scenery on its descent it is known to some Valley dwellers as "the glass elevator." For a dozen miles it runs through virgin country where rock hounds have a chance to find agates and jaspers in a region not already combed and winnowed by others.

This byway offers a new route into the Anza-Borrego Desert State Park, southern California's colorful wasteland preserve and one that grows in population each season.

From Warner Springs, across an arm of the southward-rising Volcan Mountains, into the upper end of the San Felipe drainage, into Montezuma Valley and beyond, through Ranchita, a strong pattern of history lies on the land.

The Indians have lived here for more seasons than their timeless song sagas can tell. Their marks are everywhere: names on the land and bedrock mortars in the hills.

Up from the southern desert and Carrizo and Vallecito in 1782 came the Spanish explorers under the banner of Pedro Fages. Then for more than a half century the country dozed. In 1846 General Stephen Watts Kearny crowded his Dragoons along this route on their way to do battle at fateful San Pasqual.

119

The next year, in 1847, he was followed by Colonel Philip St. George Cooke and his Mormon Battalion.

When the Gold Rush flamed thousands found their course to California and the Mother Lode across the southern route, up through the Carizzo corridor, into the San Felipe, to Warner's and on to San Gabriel and the northern mines.

The Butterfield Overland Mail hammered through this country briefly but it left an indelible mark. By then the waters at Warner's were famous and the Indians had been reckoned with more than once.

After the Civil War and the demise of the Butterfield operation the area slept again.

It was the search for gold that brought men back.

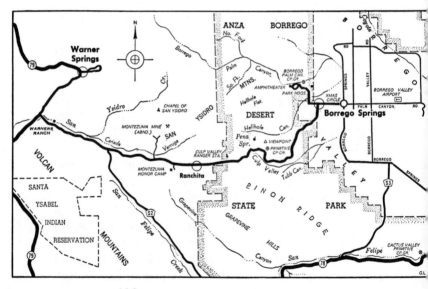

South of Warner's, on the south slope of the San Ysidro Mountains, the Montezuma Mines were discovered in 1890.

The mines were first prospected by the Rice Brothers of Warner Springs and others. They staked out the Bertha, Bonnie Bell, Hillside, Little Granite, Morning Star, Pine Ridge, Sundown and Valley View.

By about 1910, with production never outstanding, these mines were relocated, reorganized into the Montezuma Mines, the Buckeye group, and the Maid of Erin group. The Grubstake and the Lucky Strike are dated in the 1930's.

Today the tunnels are caved in and even the State Mineralogist has no accurate picture of the underground workings.

But people were in the land now; they homesteaded, chopped ranchland from the chaparral, planted orchards and dug wells.

Our byway runs south from Warner Springs on State Highway 79 a little over three miles to a road junction. Here we turn south and almost immediately pass the old Warner Ranch.

Here the old Butterfield Stage Station has been gradually falling into ruin.

A couple of years ago the two adjacent buildings were put behind an ugly chain link fence. But the vandals that are destroying these old adobes are time and the weather. One great adobe wall on the west side of the stage station has collapsed and has been dissolved by rain. The rest of the edifice will follow soon, I'm afraid, unless heroic salvage measures are implemented. The fence is not going to preserve this old way station nor will the bright new plaque be much consolation to historians when the adobe walls have all fallen and melted away.

There was a controversy a few years back about the actual location of this Butterfield Stage station. There is an old store building—also adobe—a mile or so south of the Warner's Ranch. This, the Wilson store, was the center of a small 1863 community called Kimballville. Since the Butterfield stage ran

The old Butterfield stage station at
Warner's Ranch is behind a chain link fence now,
but wind and weather are taking their toll
of the old building.

through the area two years before Kimballville was established, the late William Lawton Wright of Glendale established that the older Warner's outpost, not the Wilson store, was the Butterfield way station.

But the Wilson store is also a historic site. It still bears the plaque that incorrectly proclaims it the Butterfield station. The old Wilson store has suffered, too, from the relentless pounding of wind and weather. A protecting fence is down and cattle scratch themselves against the crumbling building.

South of this pastoral setting the road forks. If you turn left at the junction you will reach an Honor Farm, Ranchita and . . . Borrego Springs.

For this is the beginning of the spectacular new road into Borrego Springs. It saves more than a half hour going from Warner's to the center of Borrego Springs, Christmas Circle.

So turn left there, along the Cañada Verruga, and run through a magnificent stand of live oaks. To the north are the Montezuma Mines, the Los Coyotes Indian Reservation, and the uplift of the San Ysidro Mountains.

Bottle seekers have combed the mine dumps and have prowled the old homesteads in the Montezuma Valley-Ranchita area— most of them vanished and lost to memory. Even the Volcan Mountains to the southwest have yielded strange old water bottles, the glass full of bubbles, rough and irregular.

At a cattle guard across our byway a dirt road turns south into the Anza-Borrego State Park's Grapevine Canyon. It is a rough and rugged drive for a passenger car, but possible.

Then the Honor Farm whose residents helped build the road down into Borrego.

Stop at the tiny community of Ranchita. Here is a gas station, store and post office—the latter probably the smallest in San Diego County if not in the state.

Across flatland, some of it heart-breakingly cleared in years

123

A typical stretch of the newer road from Montezuma Valley-Ranchita down into Borrego Valley. The high ridge to the right is called Pinyon Ridge: Indians lived here.

past by hopeful ranchers who have since abandoned their places, our byway runs east. The San Ysidros to the north climb, grow rockier. Here is the Chimney Rock Ranch with the tall rock pile that is its namesake standing plain and clear.

Just as the road begins to descend we come to the boundary of the Anza-Borrego Desert State Park—nearly a half million acres of desert and desert-mountain lands.

A short distance beyond, on the left, is the Culp Valley Ranger Station. Stop to ask questions about the road ahead, about camping facilities in the park, about the history of the country. You'll get cheerful answers and the view from the ranger outpost is magnificent.

To the south is the pine-fringed barrier of Piñon Ridge with the Grapevine Hills beyond. To the north, closer at hand, stand the craggy San Ysidros. To the east yawns the great basin of the Borrego Valley. Beyond, on clear winter days you can see the metallic sheen of the Salton Sea. On crisper, clearer days the Chocolate Mountains, the Algodones Sand Dunes, all are visible here.

The new road into Borrego Valley was started in 1955. In June, 1964, with ceremonies, it was opened to the public and traffic on it has been brisk ever since.

From the Culp Valley east the road is high gear, there are frequent turnouts—though somehow not enough—for panoramas of the valley below.

The Ranger station at Culp Valley was established. A jeep trail, known as the Jasper road in honor of a local pioneer rancher, cuts south toward the Grapevine Canyon road. It is not recommended for passenger cars; vehicles longer than a jeep will have trouble getting through a narrow turn between a pair of giant boulders. The rocky obstacle is a nuisance but park officials feel that it adds color to the jeep drive and are reluctant to blast the giants out of the way.

*A craggy arm of the San Ysidro Mountains hangs
over the new road into the Borrego Valley region.*

Careful on-foot explorers of this area may find some fine Indian relics, but it is unlawful to collect them within the state park. Deep, painstakingly fashioned mortars have been found along the mountain ridges where the Indians once ground pinyon nuts, acorns, and mesquite beans. Ollas, great earthenware pots, are found less frequently. A museum of such findings will one day be established in the state park in Borrego Springs.

From the sumac- and boulder-decorated hills of Culp Valley the road edges down. Here is a side road on the left that leads north to Pena Spring—take the left hand fork to the dirt byway. The right hand fork leads to an impressive overlook down into Hellhole Canyon and Hellhole Flat. A pair of park rangers (and their wives) recently hiked up into a rugged tributary of Hellhole Canyon and discovered a hitherto unknown grove of palms— fifty trees probably never visited by white men. Such dramatic finds as this lend a perpetually exciting air to the Anza-Borrego country.

The water at Pena Springs is good and sweet. It bubbles vigorously all year, provides water for some cattle that graze here and drinking water for local residents such as the folks at the Culp ranger station. There are plans for development of the primitive camp here.

Staghorn cactus and their sentinel agave mark the descent into the desert country.

Borrego was all raw desert once—now it has been turned into great square patches of crops and orchards. Desert homes and their access roads paint interesting patterns on the land.

At one of the turnouts the folks of Borrego have placed a large tank of water. Going down here is no problem, but while the road is high gear, it is a stiff climb coming out of the Valley and some older cars get over-heated and thirsty.

At the first intersection on the floor of the Borrego Valley, turn left. This road leads back to the Anza-Borrego Desert State

127

*The rocky San Ysidro Mountains stand
dramatically behind the entrance to the
headquarters of the Anza-Borrego
Desert State Park.*

Park headquarters, their large Borrego Palm Canyon Campground, trailer camp and picnic area. There is a fine nature trail from the campground up into Palm Canyon and the grove of palms. Hiking distance about one and a half miles.

Other major campgrounds are at Tamarisk Grove, Bow Willow, and Split Mountain. Smaller, more primitive campgrounds are scattered throughout this park that never has too many campers. Park rules allow you to camp in almost any of the desert washes. Open fires are not allowed but you may use your own gasoline stove, brazier, hibachi, etc. The gathering of wood for fuel is prohibited.

Rangers constantly and systematically patrol the desert area. It is almost impossible to get lost. Visitors who have commented ruefully that they have camped in some remote spot for several days and have not seen a ranger are liable to be told their daily routines in detail by a ranger who had patrolled thoroughly but unobtrusively.

This is magnificent winter exploring country. It can get cool by night, but the days are a delight. And the evening sky is a bold painting of incandescent spots against inky black backdrop.

Take time to stop at the gas stations and little stores along the way, to talk to the people about the old roads, the old mines, the early homesteaders. Learning the land makes any trip more interesting.

Picture Pena Spring as an Indian watering hole, put bighorn sheep on the high points of rock as you drop down into Borrego Springs (they *are* seen here once in a while) and visualize the Spanish explorers who took foot soldiers through this endless sprawl of land.

Mostly, enjoy this new byway through unspoiled, unmarred country. Fences are few, there are no billboards in the state park and the cloud-marked sky is almost without end.

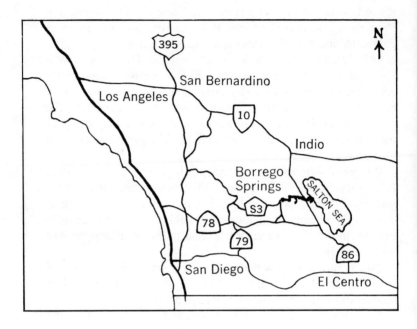

XI THE TRUCKHAVEN TRAIL — PAVED NOW AND UNIQUE

*You can hurry and see this piece of desert in an
hour; take your time and it is a day's trip. It's
the best by late winter and early springtime.*

THERE IS A FAIRLY NEW arm of pavement that skirts the southern foot of the Santa Rosa Mountains in the northeast corner of
the Anza-Borrego Desert State Park and it is best explored by
winter and early spring.

Then the weather is an ally. The haze of late summer and fall
is levered away by an impatient wind. The secret-hiding Santa
Rosas stand clear, etched with a sharper acid, close enough to
touch even though they are a mile distant in places. The ocotillo
sentinels that stand guard on the stony parade ground here are
drawn with a fine gauge pen. The pale-green explosion of the
palo verde is accented. The walls of the many washes, which
escape from the edge of the pavement and scurry and worm
away to hide under protective cliffsides, are defined by a persuasive burin. The distant bulk of hill and cliff and mountain
swell and peak is deliberate and pronounced. It is the season to
glory in the line drawing: shadows that bite, contrast of bright
and dark against the eye. Out along the new Truckhaven Trail,
to the directed eye, there are things to see, experiences to savor.
The winter wind has assured you of this.

By contrast, and regardless of the wind, you can hurry along
this avenue, from Pegleg's magical cairn to the Holly House
motel complex on State 86, and see nothing but the ocotillo
sentries.

The Anza-Borrego is wait-awhile country. You are bidden by
the old gods to walk in the washes, to ponder the meanderings

131

of the ciliated sand beetle and the pinacate, to lunch on a sandy bench where harmless grit may be blown into your sandwich by an antic wind.

There are frequent turnouts along this new Truckhaven Trail; places to park and get out and walk the rocky plains.

Some old-timers may complain about the new Truckhaven Trail. The old one, they will insist, had more character, more adventure, more hazards. And they are correct.

But the old Truckhaven Trail was essentially a jeep track. I explored it in the old days in a jeep. There was an easy run out to the turnoff to Fonts Point, and a safe but sandy run down to the Point where an incredible view of the badlands could be had. Beyond that the road got rougher. The side canyons invited, just are they do now. You could jeep up to them just so far, and beyond that, as now, you had to walk. There were steep pitches down and out of washes. There was washboard. A passenger car would have had trouble with much of it.

Today it is paved and wide and straightened and leveled. It is sort of antiseptic—though mainly in comparison—until you consider the country you are crossing.

Now it comes alive. The washes, snaking away both to the north and the south, take on a beckoning charm. Erosion is an element of beauty here in the deep-cut canyons and the fluted cliffs. Study the rocks that make walking difficult in some places: concretions, eroded rocks, gemstones, and the ring of worn stones from an old Indian house.

The Anza-Borrego Desert State Park, which is plastered up against the overhang of Riverside County and against the western wall of Imperial County, occupies a good portion of desert San Diego County.

There are many delights in this state park, one of my favorites of all in the system.

Here you can camp in any wash your car will take you to. You can explore away from the ruts of the man who went before. Lost? You'll never achieve it. The ranger-patrolmen of the Anza-Borrego have a knack that reminds one of the Royal Canadian Mounties. People just don't get lost, or into much trouble, in the Anza-Borrego. Someone shows up with jeep and tow cable and radio and smile before worry juices can build. The Anza-Borrego has many legends. The one I like the best is the continuing saga of the ranger-patrolmen. Trust them.

From Borrego Springs head east from Christmas Circle along Palm Canyon Road. It's roughly four and half miles east to Pegleg Road. You drive north on this, up toward Coyote Mountain and the waiting Santa Rosas.

Watch out for the Santa Rosas. They will snare you with their hidden places and lost springs. They will sing to you to come and explore. Stopper your ears unless you have unlimited time. It is a song they sing very well.

At the end of Pegleg Road you'll come to the Pegleg Smith Monument. In 1949, according to Horace Parker's fine *Anza-Borrego Desert Guide Book,* a group of desert cronies—Harry Oliver, John Hilton, Ed DuVall, Harry Woods and Doc Beaty—fashioned the cairn of rocks that would be the Pegleg Monument.

Pegleg Smith, the prospector the desert fan club was honoring, was the old one-legged gentleman who, according to a richer legend, once found a butte dotted with strange black stones. These turned out to be oxidized nuggets of gold and more than one tall-tale-teller since has insisted he has found the lode.

Most people believe otherwise, some doubt the whole legend while insisting that it be perpetuated. You can look for Pegleg's butte if you've a hankering while you are in the Anza-Borrego. The rangers will tell you where others have looked. They'll drink your celebration champagne if you find the bonanza and will ask nothing more.

It is at the Pegleg Monument that the new Truckhaven trace

*The new Truckhaven Trail is a wide paved
highway, a high speed thoroughfare reaching
from Pegleg's Monument in Borrego Valley
to Highway 86 near the Salton Sea.
But it's more fun just to poke along.*

starts. The Anza-Borrego staff have issued a self-guiding auto tour folder, which they'll hand you (if they haven't run out again) when you come to call.

This folder will tell you that at 3.6 miles from the monument you'll come to the turnoff south to Fonts Point.

Check with a ranger before you drive this sandy track four and a half miles south to an impressive overlook of the badlands.

It is a drive that you'll enjoy. The overlook is impressive and the badlands will give moon explorers nightmares. But the course has sandy spots that can grab your tires if the road conditions are just so. After a rain, when the sand is packed down, the drive is usually a piece of cake. Other times—well, don't worry, a ranger-patrolman will be along to pry you out of the sand trap in good time.

About seven-tenths of a mile farther along the Truckhaven avenue—and you'll note, please, that it is labeled "The Borrego-Salton Seaway," a rather dreadful substitute for the Truckhaven Trail—you'll come to a viewpoint. This one commands the Clark Dry Lake Area to the north, a playa tucked in between Coyote Mountain and the skirt of the Santa Rosas.

Seven and one-tenth miles from Pegleg's monument you'll find Palo Verde Wash. Here you'll discover the delicately colored palo verde trees, one of the joys of the arid region.

Get out of your car here and walk the wash. It was here, one day by winter, that we spent a half-hour following a ciliated sand beetle and a pinacate on their sandy wanderings. It was the the desert in microcosm. Their presence puts a lie to the word that the desert is not an alive place. Not alive? Study the green leaf explosion along the whip arms of the ocotillo; by early spring that green offering will stand in giddy contrast to the bright red of the ocotillo blossoms. As brilliant a testimony of life as you could find anywhere.

A rough jeep road here marches north to Palo Verde Spring.

This watering spot is in bighorn sheep country. Watch for them if you are jeeping. A glimpse of this shy desert animal is a souvenir of the Anza-Borrego that few have taken home.

From a point 8.7 miles from the Pegleg stone pile is a viewpoint south into the badlands. Mark well that mammoth and prehistoric horse walked here once; evidences have been found. Study the rain-etched washes, dramatic extravagances of nature in a static land.

Smoke Tree Wash stands along the road just beyond. The smoke tree is another happy desert dweller. In the proper light, and with the viewer in the proper mood, the generosity of the smoke tree's purpled foliage looks almost like smoke along a sandy wash.

You can see pieces of the old Truckhaven Trail as you make your eastward passage: knotty pieces of road that spooked strangers to the desert and delighted the faithful. Doc Beaty, an old Anza-Borrego resident, fashioned the shortcut road from Borrego Springs east to present Highway 86 in 1929.

Eleven and four-tenths miles from Pegleg's monument is Cannonball Wash. Below, southeast, is the Pumpkin Patch. The colorful language indicates that there are rock concretions here, headsized and bigger, that resemble pumpkins and cannonballs. You'll have to walk some distance to see much of the outcroppings. Best aid here is Parker's Paisano Press edition of the *Anza-Borrego Desert Guide Book*. You'll find detailed information on the Pumpkin Patch in Parker's volume.

Another mile and you come to a spot where you can look due east, and if the winey wind is at work, you can make out the distant shoreline of the depression-trapped Salton Sea.

Off to the north is the jeep road, and a rough one, back to John Hilton's World War II calcite crystal mining area. If you have the time, hike in the area for a distance. You'll find some uncommon desert landscape.

Then on the byway you'll find yourself in a kind of civilization. You've passed a microwave tower, you've crossed into Imperial County, you've discovered a golf course on the desert, then houses, finally Holly House and Highway 86.

Follow ahead on Marina Drive and you'll come to the beach eventually. You'll find boats and fishermen and trailer parks and marinas.

The Salton Sea is almost ringed with such commerce today. It stands in sharp contrast to the dusty and arid peace of the deep desert. The main thrills I have experienced in the Salton Sea country were searching for and finding the browned edge of the old shoreline of Lake Cahuilla (Blakes Sea, Lake Le Conte), the prehistoric ocean that once stood here.

You have driven the new Truckhaven Trail now, the paved version of Doc Beaty's old jeep course.

For your visit I wish you a 100-mile horizon and a covey of cumulus on the distant edge of sky.

I entreat you to be patient in your exploration of the new Truckhaven Trail. Don't hurry. At best you have 20 miles to examine. If you started early in the morning you could walk the whole span of it by dark.

So use the turnouts, park and get out of the car and look for waterworn stones and camouflaged lizards and winter greenery.

Rain works magic in the desert, and you'll find blades of ephemeral grass and hints of belly flowers brightening the sandy washes and benches.

Do not regard this arid world as bleak, blank-map stuff. The ocotillo that grows here had a reason for picking this place to cast its spiny shadow. The creosote bush is in harmony with the rubbly flatland. This is true, deep-desert country, and the washes that run exploding with brown-frothed water by winter only serve to nurture the glorious palo verde and smoke trees.

This is the Borrego-Salton Seaway and its paved grandeur is

only as old as last April. Along it, later in the spring, you'll find a dazzling display of diminutive wildflowers. By summer it is fiery along this course. Fall brings a haze over the land. By winter, that haze is gone and the monochromatic wilderness is at its best.

You can drive the new Truckhaven Trail's 20 miles in 20 minutes if you've a mind for speed. Many people do. But then, to them, the desert is nothing but sand and drab and lonesomeness.

We, who have heard the sad music seeping down from the mystic Santa Rosas, know better.

This view by the author is of the old Truckhaven Trail, a jeep course for much of its run. It was, at times, sandy, rough and washboarded. The Santa Rosa Mountains stand in the background.

XII UP AND OUT OF THE ANZA-BORREGO STATE PARK

Best explored by cool weather. The off-pavement
side roads are no great problem and remember, the
Anza-Borrego park rangers keep a sharp eye on everything.

THE WINTER sun that rides high over the lower Anza-Borrego wasteland is filtered through yards of beige gossamer that dyes the sun-illuminated landscape tones of buff and yellow and ochre.

The land is a monotony of color. Nothing moves. The road that travels this land of a single hue is a dusty elastic band that stretches from horizon to horizon, and even the rising dust is the same color, repeated mile after mile.

But look again.

Already the ocotillo is at work putting out green leaflets along its long pencil of spines. Tiny and green, they sparkle, jewel-like. There's a promise of buds on the cactus. A hint of yellow blossoms on the desert plants. If it is winter—tomorrow will be the time of blossoming.

And movement. Pause for a second and the desert shimmers with it. In the burned grass that blur of angled pattern is a road-runner out hunting. On that dead agave a young hawk is perched, head pivoting, waiting for the hidden rodent to skitter once more. Lizards dart and beetles scar the sugary sand. Little anonymous birds, some so insignificant you could hold half a dozen, full-feathered, in your fist, winnow seeds from the sterile gravels.

Follow the line of the road through the land and look higher than the lace of dust left behind by the last car, to seek the horizon. See the dot. It is a golden eagle on scout.

From Scissors Crossing, where County Highway S2 crosses State Highway 78, south on S2 to U.S. Highway 80, this is a

139

burned land. But there is drama here, painted in pastels, hidden behind a frieze of dead grass, poised in the chiffon sky. It takes a certain patience to seek it out, but the find is nourishing.

S2, in its move south, travels through land that is anchored in history and legend. Here is Earthquake Valley and off to the southwest, bulking and close at hand, are the Oriflamme Mountains. There is a story, not heard so much anymore, but coming back into vogue, that ghost lights one time played on the Oriflammes—spectral illuminations that glowed where there were

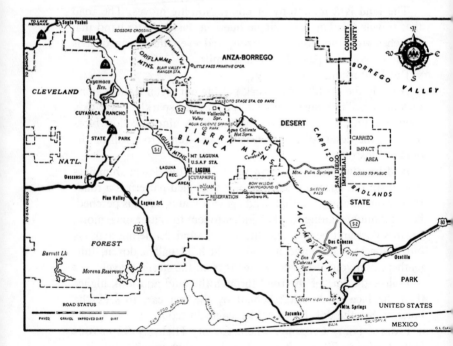

no cabins, no campers. It is an eerie yarn to spin during evenings at campgrounds along the byway route, say at Little Pass Primitive Camp, near the Oriflammes and across the road from the Blair Valley ranger station.

This is the Anza-Borrego Desert State Park now, an immense tract of desert land hammered down around burned hills and cut by a thousand washes. It is a preserve where ocotillo and cholla and beavertail and creosote bushes reign and where coyotes and bobcats and bighorn sheep move among them.

This road—S2—is called the Old Overland Stage Route, and over at least part of its passage the old Butterfield Overland Mail ran on its way from St. Louis to San Francisco. The historic route ran from Yuma west, up across the terrible sandy Carizzo country to Agua Caliente, Vallecito, Box Canyon and north to Scissors Crossing and on to Warners. That was between 1858 and 1861, more than a hundred years ago or only yesterday. The course up Box Canyon can still be walked. An historic marker calls attention to the area. You can see where freighters chopped away the stone walls of the narrow defile to make room for wagons in the early days.

More than the Overland Mail passed this way: there were soldiers and emigrants and gold seekers. The latter came by the thousands and left the track fouled and stinking with the carcasses of dead animals. Historians still find the crumble of broken wagon wheels in the wastelands, the jumble of junked harness chain.

It is a good road, this S2, all the way south. At times you travel through fields of prickly cholla and lean ocotillo. At times there is grass standing on the alluvials that reach down from the Tierra Blancas. Staghorn cactus looks delicate and touchable; touch it and it wounds you unforgivingly.

Walk the desert floor away from the highway. Study the ground intently. Even by winter there will be belly flowers, tiny,

The restored stage station at Vallecito, a county park on the edge of the Anza-Borrego Desert State Park. Vallecito was once a stage stop along the old Butterfield Overland Mail line.

almost invisible plant life: roots and leaves and brilliant blossome. Insects, just as tiny, traffic in pollen in this dwarf universe.

The furry beetle you see, wandering aimlessly around pebble and plant, is the ciliated sand beetle. His fur helps him survive under the summer sun. Another beetle that crawls here is the glossy pinacate bug, a silly fellow who will stand on his head in confusion if you touch him with your toe. Harm them not, they are all part of the desert scheme of life—each necessary to the other.

It was deep winter when last we came this way, and a spot of white on the desert plain moved. With field glasses we could see it was some sort of large predator bird, with curved beak and talons. It waited, chaperoned by tiny birds that make this part of the desert their home, until its prey showed itself. Then there was a scramble, a darting, the little birds showered up, the white-breasted hunter struck and flew away with something dangling from a claw. The park ranger later identified the bird for us as a young eagle.

The route from Earthquake Valley stepladders gently down to the main floor of the desert. Blair Valley is lower than Earthquake, and Vallecito Valley is lower than Blair. There are private trailer camps along the road, and at Vallecito, a restored stage station and campground. It is operated as a county park— you are in a peninsula of private land outside the Anza-Borrego Desert State Park here. Then you move back into the park and travel south to Agua Caliente.

For years there have been legends about the curative powers of the waters of Agua Caliente. If you are a resident of San Diego County and your doctor certifies that you need this therapy, you can live at Agua Caliente on a semi-permanent basis, soaking in the 98-degree mineral waters. The county park here is well-tended and attractive, though barren, and during the winter it is not always easy to get a campsite. There is a charge.

143

The highway through the Laguna Mountains Recreation Area is marked by stately black oaks, tall conifers.

The good highway moves on south from Agua Caliente, passes the Canebreak Canyon area, where there are a handful of desert homes—some little more than shacks. Again the park boundary has jogged, allowing such a development on private land.

Here, within the park, is the turnoff to the west into Mountain Palm Springs. Take this drive. The road is sandy, but if you stay in the ruts you will have no trouble. Seek the parking area on the hill to the north; do not attempt to cross the sandy wash at the end of the road.

From the hill you can look north and and see the first of several groves of palms in the area. It is a short walk back to them. Follow the watercourse for a mile or so and you'll find other palm groves, hidden from the road. They are one of the miracles of the desert, plants so large drawing enough moisture from this arid land.

Off to the east, where you can go only if you have a jeep, you'll see the wall of the Carrizo Badlands. For further exploration in the area—off the highway—get a copy of Horace Parker's *Anza-Borrego Desert Guide Book*. It explains all the deep desert's secrets in detail.

On down S2 now brings the byway explorer to Bow Willow Campground. A mile-long side road runs west to this site and the area ranger station. This is a dry camp—bring your own water. There are only ten camping units here, and they are frequently filled on winter weekends. You'd do better to arrive on Friday. You can stay two weeks if you've a mind to.

What do you do in a desert campground?

By days there are little hikes you can take to acquaint yourself with the desert flora and fauna. A mountain lion passed through Bow Willow not long ago and left tracks in the wash. Bobcats have been seen. Rabbits run through the cactus. There is an assortment of birds. Some of the washes that reach out from the low hills are great to explore.

By night, with a campfire and good coffee for cheer, study the stars. Were there ever so many before, or so close? That star that moves on a straight line is probably a man-made satellite (one of ours or one of theirs?), and in the course of a long evening of watching, you are apt to see more than one.

Local rangers make it a habit of visiting campers in the evening, will happily fill in on local lore and legend. Anza-Borrego is a gigantic park, and the rangers here have a limitless store of tales to tell. Encourage them to talk.

South now from Bow Willow's charms, up Sweeney Pass and down to the turnoff to Dos Cabezas. The road back to the track and the old station of the San Diego and Arizona Eastern Railway (it runs from San Diego via Tijuana and Mexico to the Imperial Valley) is not paved, but again you'll have no trouble if you stay in the ruts. The park people may improve this natural and attractive camping area one day.

And then on south along S2 to Ocotillo, a strange little community in the desert depths, and U.S. Highway 80.

To make a loop trip with strong geographic contrasts on this byway excursion, drive west now along U.S. 80. You'll find it is freeway-like for many miles. Be sure to stop at the desert tower near Mountain Springs for a vantage-point look at the desert to the east.

On west then, thirty-odd miles to Laguna Junction, the spot where the road from the Laguna Mountains Recreation Area touches U.S. 80. If the desert was warm on the days you called, you'll find the Lagunas cool, perhaps even frosty. Snow often visits them by winter, and as a rule most of the Cleveland National Forest's campgrounds are closed. But here and there you'll find one open where you can pause and brew a pot of coffee.

The pines will be at their healthiest now. The Kellogg oaks will have lost their leaves that were so brilliantly colored in November and December. There are a number of resorts where you can stop for refreshments if you wish.

The road passes the Mt. Laguna Air Force Station—you'll see the white radar domes for miles before you get to them.

On the ride near the radar station is a fine viewpoint from which you can look deep into the Anza-Borrego country you just left. The dominant peak out there, riding like a ship in the sea of single color, is Sombrero Peak. Bighorn sheep have been spotted on its flanks. Nearer at hand is the Cuyapaipe Indian Reservation.

On north our byway runs through beautiful conifer country to a meeting with the Cuyamaca State Park road at Cuyamaca Reservoir. Farther north is Julian, the fairest of the San Diego County's mountain communities. The museum in Julian is open each weekend, and it houses an assortment of area treasures.

Another suggestion: between Julian and Santa Ysabel you'll find a collection of apple stores. Stop here for new crop apples, nuts and sweet cider.

From Santa Ysabel you can return home via Ramona, or north past Lake Henshaw and Pauma Valley and Pala, or north through Warner and Aguanga.

What you have seen this day is a vivid scenic mixture of San Diego County's backcountry. For such excellent roads, such as S2 and the Laguna Mountain course, we have to be thankful to state and county planners. For the places along the way to stop for gasoline, food, cold drinks and hot coffee, we must nod to private industry.

But for the excitements of the land, for the young eagle out hunting, the pinacate beetle standing on its head, for the belly flowers and the green blush of leafing ocotillo, for the resinous scent of chapparral and the sharp perfume of pine, for the night with the stars and the walks that net a glimpse of bobcat, we have to thank a bountiful nature.

BIBLIOGRAPHY

Bailey, Paul. *Walkara, Hawk of the Mountains*. Los Angeles: Westernlore Press, 1954.

Bailey, Richard C. *Explorations in Kern*. Bakersfield, Calif.: Kern County Historical Society, 1959.

Beattie, George William, and Helen Pruitt Beattie. *Heritage of the Valley*. Oakland, Calif.: Biobooks, 1951.

Campbell, Elizabeth W. Crozer. *An Archaeological Survey of the Twenty Nine Palms Region*. Highland Park, Los Angeles, Southwest Museum Papers Number Seven, Southwest Museum, 1931.

Campbell, Elizabeth W. Crozer, and William H. Campbell. *The Pinto Basin Site*. Highland Park, Los Angeles, Southwest Museum Papers Number Nine, Southwest Museum, 1935.

Chalfant, W. A. *Death Valley, The Facts*. Stanford: Stanford University Press, 1930.

Edwards, E. I. *Desert Voices*. Los Angeles: The Westernlore Press, 1958.

_____. *Freeman's, A Stage Stop on the Mojave*. Glendale: La Siesta Press, 1964.

_____. *Lost Oases Along the Carrizo*. Los Angeles, Calif.: The Westernlore Press, 1961.

Grant, Campbell, and James W. Baird and K. Kenneth Pringle. *Rock Drawings of the Coso Range*. China Lake, Calif. Maturango Museum (Publication Number 4), 1968.

Gudde, Erwin G. *California Place Names*. Berkeley: University of California Press, 1960.

Hine, Robert V. *California's Utopian Colonies*. San Marino: Huntington Library, 1953.

Holmes, Roger, and Paul Bailey. *Fabulous Farmer*. Los Angeles: Westernlore Press, 1956.

Hubbard, Paul B. *Garlock Memories*. Ridgecrest, Calif.: Hubbard Printing, 1960.

Indian Wells Valley Handbook. China Lake, Calif.: The China Lake Branch of the American Association of University Women, 1960.

Jaeger, Edmund C. *The California Deserts*. Stanford: Stanford University Press, 1965.

Kirk, Ruth. *Exploring Death Valley*. Stanford: Stanford University Press, 1956, 1965.

148

Kroeber, A. L. *Handbook of the Indians of California*. Berkeley, Calif.: California Book Co., Ltd., 1953.

Layne, J. Gregg. *Western Wayfaring*. Los Angeles: Automobile Club of Southern California, 1954.

Leadabrand, Russ. *A Guidebook to the Mojave Desert*. Los Angeles, Calif.: The Ward Ritchie Press, 1966.

——————. *Westways,* various articles. Los Angeles: Automobile Club of Southern California.

Lee, Bourke. *Death Valley*. New York: The Macmillan Co., 1930.

——————. *Death Valley Men*. New York: The Macmillan Co., 1932.

Lee, W. Storrs. *The Great California Deserts*. New York: G. P. Putnam's Sons, 1962.

Los Angeles Corral of the Westerners. *Brand Book Number 11*. Los Angeles, 1964.

Miller, Ronald Dean. *Mines of the High Desert*. Glendale, Calif.: La Siesta Press, 1965.

Mitchell, Roger. *Exploring Joshua Tree*. Glendale, Calif.: La Siesta Press, 1964.

Myrick, David F. *Railroads of Nevada and Eastern California*. Berkeley, Calif.: Howell-North, Vol. I, 1962.

——————. *Railroads of Nevada and Eastern California*. Berkeley, Calif.: Howell-North, Vol. II, 1963.

O'Neal, Lulu Rasmussen. *A Peculiar Piece of Desert*. Los Angeles: Westernlore Press, 1957.

Parker, Horace. *Anza/Borrego Desert Guide Book,* Third Edition. Balboa Island, Calif.: Paisano Press, 1969.

Peirson, Erma. *Kern's Desert*. Bakersfield, Calif.: Kern County, Historical Society, 1956.

Publications of the California Historical Society, San Francisco, Calif., various dates.

Publications of the Historical Society of Southern California, Los Angeles, Calif., various dates.

Robinson, W. W. *The Story of San Bernardino County*. San Bernardino: Pioneer Title Insurance Co., 1958.

Settle, Glen A. *Here Roamed the Antelope*. Kern-Antelope Historical Society, Inc., 1963.

Smith, Gerald A., and Clifford J. Walker. *Indian Slave Trade Along the Mojave Trail*. San Bernardino, Calif.: San Bernardino County Museum, 1965.

State Mineralogist, *Mines and Mineral Resources*. San Francisco: California State Mining Bureau, 1916.

The Story of the Pacific Coast Borax Co. Los Angeles: Ward Ritchie Press, 1951.

Thompson, David G. *The Mohave Desert Region, California.* Water-Supply Paper 578, Washington, D.C., United States Department of the Interior, 1929.

Weight, Harold O. *Lost Mines of Death Valley.* Twentynine Palms, Calif.: The Calico Press, 1953, 1961.

Westerners, Los Angeles Corral, Russ Leadabrand, Editor: *Brand Book Number 11.* Los Angeles, Calif.: The Ward Ritchie Press, 1964.

Wilson, Neill C. *Silver Stampede.* New York: The Macmillan Co., 1937.

Wynn, Marcia Rittenhouse. *Desert Bonanza.* Glendale, Calif.: The Arthur H. Clark Co., 1963.

INDEX

151

153